Corporate

Cyberwar

Author: Dr. Michael Teng

Published in 2011 by

Corporate Turnaround Centre Pte Ltd.

Printed in Singapore

By : JCS Digital Solutions Pte Ltd

About the Author

Dr. Teng is widely recognized as a turnaround CEO in Asia by the news media. He has been interviewed on the international media on many occasions on the subject of corporate turnaround and transformation as well as Internet marketing such as the Malaysian Business Radio, BFM 89-9, News Radio FM 93.8, Malaysian Business Radio, Edge Radio (USA), the Channel News Asia, the Boss Magazine, Economic Bulletin, the Today, World Executive Digest, Lianhe ZaoPao, StarBiz and the Straits Times. Success University and SkyquestCom broadcast his online seminars globally to 120 countries.

Dr. Mike Teng is the author of a best-selling book *"Corporate Turnaround: Nursing a Sick Company Back to Health",* in 2002 which is also translated into the Bahasa, Indonesia and Mandarin. Management guru Professor Philip Kotler and business tycoons Mr. Oei Hong Leong and Dr. YY Wong endorse his book. He has subsequently authored more than twenty three management books. Three of the books are on Internet marketing.

Dr. Teng is currently the Managing Director of Corporate Turnaround Centre Pte Ltd (www.corporateturnaroundcentre.com), which provides corporate training and management advisory services in Singapore, Malaysia, Vietnam, Ghana, etc. He is the national trainer appointed by the Singapore government to train displaced senior managers and deploy them to run SMEs.

He has more than 29 years of experience in starting new plants, strategic planning, and operational management responsibilities in the Asia Pacific region. Of these, he held Chief Executive Officer positions for 19 years in multi-national and publicly listed companies. He was the CEO of a U.S. MNC based in Singapore for ten years. He spearheaded the turnaround of several troubled companies. He also advised several boards of directors of publicly listed companies.

Dr. Teng served as an Executive Council member for fourteen years and the last four years as the President of the Marketing Institute of Singapore (2000 – 2004), the national marketing association. He is the President of the National University Singapore MBA Alumni and University of South Australia Alumni.

Dr. Teng holds a Doctorate in Business Administration (DBA) from the University of South Australia, a Master of Business Administration (MBA) and Bachelor of Mechanical Engineering (BEng) from the National University of Singapore. He is also a Professional Engineer (P Eng, Singapore), Chartered Engineer (C Eng, UK) and Fellow Member of several prestigious professional institutes, namely Chartered Institute of Marketing (FCIM), Chartered Management Institute (FCMI), Institute of Mechanical Engineers (FIMechE), Marketing Institute of Singapore (FMIS), Institute of Electrical Engineers (FIEE) and Senior Member of Singapore Computer Society (SMSCS). He is also a Practising Management Consultant (PMC) certified by the Singapore government.

Table of Contents

An Introduction to Corporate Cyberwar

From fire and iron to i-Phones and fuel cells, technologies have always had great impacts on the course of civilization. New technologies have enabled us to do things that we could never have imagined. For example, who possibly could have thought of banking without going to a bank, communicating without a phone (let alone video chatting) or shopping without visiting a shop, even fifty years back? New technologies also give rise to new crafts and professions: iron and steel forged blacksmiths; the advent of ships empowered merchants, explorers and voyagers; the industrial revolution gave rise to industrialists; and the invention of computers produced a bunch of geeky coders. These new professions have prospered as the technologies that birthed them have been refined. All, however, faced serious threats due to external factors including famines, economic depressions, political unrest and, of course, wars.

Wars are widely understood to be the worst type of catastrophe that can ever happen to humanity. Although war is often used by power-hungry statesmen to ensure personal gain, more times than not destruction is the only result. Unfortunately, technologies also have facilitated wars and, thus, caused massive destruction. Since ancient times, technological innovations often have revolutionized warfare. As proof, think of stone hammers and then metal daggers, arrow-firing chariots, gunpowder, bombing aircraft and nuclear weapons. New weapons and vehicles have provided armies that possess them with great advantages and have enabled them to unleash more and more destructive assaults.

War does not occur only between states and militants. Alvin Toffler once said, "No significant socioeconomic change takes place without conflict, especially large scale, high speed economic changes." Each and every fierce competitor has been involved in some form of war. Starting with fights between opposing groups of cattlemen to modern-day office politics and corporate rivalry, the list of these small-scale wars is endless. Many of these wars have been targeted to outshine a business rival, whether by hijacking a business secret or by destroying the rival altogether. The mid-nineteenth century wars between European imperialists to gain control of new markets and resources are a prime example.

Cyberwar

Now, in the era of Internet and information technology, a huge proportion of business operations are web based. Large-volume financial transactions are done over the Internet, innumerable merchants are involved in e-business, information technology and automation are used to run factories, and for most businesses, websites act as the first point of customer service, corporate communications and promotion. These high-technology practices have increased the efficiency of the business operations and, thus, reduced costs. They also offer convenience to customers like never before. But every ride has its downside, and unfortunately, Internet business is no exception.

The spread of digital convenience has come at a cost: the cost of digital security. Networks have made communications easier. If not well guarded, however, networks, just like a highway, can be used by attackers to fast and furious effect. With increasing dependence on the Internet and other networks, our systems are being more and more exposed to potential fraud, attacks, defacements and whatnot. The threat is multifaceted, complex and frightening. Modern societies are extremely dependent on computer systems in general and on the Internet in particular. This dependence provides enemies with more avenues through which to attack. If essential infrastructure components such as banks, refineries, air-traffic-control systems and power stations should be brought down simultaneously, it would probably be the worst disaster in human history. On top of the in-built vulnerability that networks bring, the absence of well-structured laws about cyber terrorism and the complexity of tracing back processes further help the cause of cyber terrorists.

In last twenty years, enough incidents have occurred to convince users of the Internet's vulnerable nature. Starting with Titan Rain and then Moonlight Maze and progressing to WikiLeaks and Stuxnet, cyber attacks have thoroughly stirred the worldwide system from time to time. In some instances, years passed before an ongoing assault is detected. With Titan Rain, an attack went undetected for two years. In some other cases, nothing can be done against an assault, even if the attackers and the type of attack are known, as in the case of WikiLeaks. In most cases of cyber attack, tracing back the attackers is practically impossible unless they come out bragging. Yes, speculation abounds and the identity of the attackers may even be obvious, but hardly any evidence may be found with which to build a strong legal case. Cyberwar knows no boundaries. Cyber attacks have plagued systems and websites all over the world, whether in the United States, China, India or the Middle East, and they have targeted a wide variety of parties, among them government institutions, corporations, news agencies and others.

Experts widely acknowledge concerns over Internet security. William J. Lynn (Deputy Secretary of Defence, United States) stated, "As a doctrinal matter, the Pentagon has formally recognized cyberspace as a new domain in warfare . . . [which] has become just as critical to military operations as land, sea, air, and space." In his latest book, *Cyberwar*, Richard A. Clarke, a renowned defence and security expert from the United States, has defined cyberwar as "actions by a nation-state to penetrate another nation's computers or networks for the purposes of causing damage or disruption." This definition, however, may be viewed as lacking because it does not account for non-state attacks.

Corporate Cyberwar

A disturbing aspect of cyberwar is its non-discriminatory nature. In cyber space, no gaps exist between civilian and government infrastructure. Practically everything is staged on a common backbone of networks and information technology. As a result of this overlapping presence, an attack on any part of a nation's cyber infrastructure can be lethal. A worm introduced in one computer will spread to other systems via connecting networks. This vicious infection cycle continues, and a huge number of computers and websites end up being affected. A cyber attack will not only affect military and government institutions, but also civilian ones including banking, the electric grid, Internet-based supply chains, business systems and others.

On the face of it, cyberwar may look like a clash between two states or politically motivated parties, at least going by most of the examples so far. To date, most cyber assaults have been executed either *by* a state (e.g., cyber attacks on Estonia, allegedly executed by Russia) or *on* a state (e.g., Titan Rain on the United States)— exactly the same as with traditional wars fought between political powers. Still, traditional war is of deep concern for businesses, mainly because it destroys the normal business environment by creating panic, insecurity and economic turmoil. Moreover, in war, businesses may find themselves in the midst of the crossfire, which is certainly not a desirable outcome for their owners.

The case of cyberwar for businesses is similar. Don't be fooled by the apparent political character of cyberwars to this point: Corporations with significant Internet- based operations have plenty of reasons to worry. To start with, such companies may find they are caught up in a political cyber siege. Think of the case of the Middle East, where a number of Islamic protest groups are taking down the major websites of Israel, the United States, and European nations. They want to spread their viewpoint and take revenge for bloodshed in their homelands. What better way to achieve this than by attacking heavily trafficked websites and substituting for the original pages for their own carrying their own words? And that's exactly what they are doing: They are taking down one website after another, mostly those of media houses and Western service providers (e.g., eBay and other merchants, credit card providers, etc.). Similarly, WikiLeaks supporters attacked banks and credit-card websites that refused to allow transactions with the WikiLeaks website and its accounts. In both of these cases, the companies under attack had nothing to do with the political issues at hand; they simply tried to serve their clientele (in case of the Middle East) or abide by government regulations (in case of WikiLeaks). Still, the companies found themselves on the receiving end of destruction because the cyber attackers perceived them as aides and allies of their political enemies, and hence as oppressors.

Another threatening scenario occurs when one political entity (e.g., a nation) decides to turn the heat on the economy and infrastructure of another such entity. Stuxnet, the worm that took cyberspace by storm in 2010, specifically targeted infrastructure and manufacturing sectors that rely heavily on automation. Similar attacks also have been experienced in China, in South East Asia and even in the United States. Experts believe that industrial worms in the future are going to play a major role in politically motivated corporate cyberwars.

Another possible area of concern is business vs. business attacks. It's much easier for a business to attack the web presence of a rival rather than its physical infrastructure. Most of the laws governing such attacks are vague at best, tracing the origin of the attacks is virtually impossible unless the attacker is plain careless, and the impact of such an attack can be severe, meaning the attacker can inflict maximum damage with minimal risk. Much corporate espionage already has taken the Internet route, and many more acts of espionage are expected to follow.

Today's businesses face a set of complex, multifaceted risks in using the Internet and information-technology systems, and these threats are only expected to intensify in future. From a business's point of view, the most threatening aspect of Internet insecurity is its overwhelming reach. Today's businesses do not command their own fate but instead find their most strategic concerns intertwined with a variety of issues. Society's essential infrastructure (e.g., electricity, water, transport, etc.) all depends on IT-based automation. An attack on a country's infrastructure base therefore can virtually halt all of that country's businesses. A targeted attack on a website's host server can pull down a business's website for quite some time. Compromised banking information can cause unauthorized transactions from accounts. Securing a business's own networks and databases is not going to suffice any more. To evade the evils of the Internet and IT, businesses will have to adhere to safe cyber practices and choose partners more wisely than ever.

Cyberwar: Myths and Truths

Myth 1

Cyberwar is for states to think about. Businesses are safe and secure. Why should I bother?

Truth 1

Businesses are extremely vulnerable to cyber attacks. These days, most corporates have major Internet presences, use significant amounts of information technology and rely on computer systems. Each link in this chain of business can be taken down by cyberwar. A worm can cause significant damage to systems and steal classified information from business databases. The stolen data can, in turn, be used to cause huge damage to a business's reputation, operations and financials. Business websites can be defaced by exploiting their security holes. Rivals can hamper operations during peak sale seasons or sneak a peek at top-secret business strategies. Much as Wikileaks did with the world of state diplomacy, media can obtain internal reports and turn them into scoops and scandals. Once any of these occur, business owner can do practically nothing in defence. To avoid getting bogged down in unexpected cyber attacks, advance attention to the security of networks, websites and corporate computers is practically the business owner's only protection.

Myth 2

My business is too small to be a victim of cyberwar. I have other things to worry about.

Truth 2

No business is out of the reach of cyber attacks. Short of a DDoS (Distributed Denial of Service) attack on your website, most businesses are still exposed to untargeted attacks (e.g., identity frauds, fraud transactions, website defacements, etc.). Let's consider the example of a small, web-based merchant. If an attacker can make its way through the company's web portal, a lot of damage can be on the cards. The attacker can steal bank account/credit card details and make fraudulent transactions. Classified details of customers may be stolen or the website defaced to harm the company's reputation. At the very least, such an attack will stall trade and transactions over the website for a few significant days. Once it's known that the website is compromised, cleaning up the worms and scripts to get the site running well again will cost quite a few man hours (and lots of money). If such an attack has been plotted by an aggressive competitor, s/he will definitely make good use of the cleanup downtime and any information collected to gain an extra edge. For a business, small size is no security against cyberwar.

Myth 3

Fighting corporate cyberwars takes a lot of knowledge and skill. I'll leave the worries to a professional security provider, and I won't need to understand cyber risks.

Truth 3

Businesses and their owners can never wash their hands of cyber security issues, no matter who has been hired to look after the issue. Cyber security affects the most important parts of a business— data, processes, customers and, most importantly, financials. Can an outsider really be trusted completely with all of these classified items? WikiLeaks has demonstrated that trust has to be placed very carefully, and it might not be very wise to neglect that lesson. On the other hand, many security-service providers cost much more than small businesses can afford. A much cheaper solution is to use over-the-counter software tools (e.g., anti-virus and anti-spyware programmes, etc.). Learning and understanding the technical and managerial aspects of cyber attacks will still be necessary, but this may take much less effort than finding and dealing with a trustworthy security-service provider within the constraints of a small-business budget.

The next few chapters are a good place to start the process of learning about various aspects of corporate cyberwar. We shall start with a history of cyberwar in general and corporate cyberwar in particular. A discussion of how cyber attacks are executed follows, along with explanations of different cyber-attack methods, relevant technical details and how to fight back. Finally, a few golden rules to help you survive and win corporate cyberwars are provided. Brace yourself: One of the most important lessons of your life is about to begin!

A Brief History of Cyberwar

In June of 1982, at the peak of Cold War tensions, a U.S. early-warning satellite detected a huge explosion in Siberia. A little intelligence gathering soon revealed that the incident was nothing but an explosion on one of the U.S.S.R's gas pipelines. The cause was a malfunction of the control system that Soviet agents had hijacked from a Canadian firm. What they didn't know was that the CIA had already tampered with the stolen software. In his memoirs, Thomas Reed, an ex–secretary of the air force, wrote rather proudly about this piece of counterespionage. According to him, the intention was to make the Soviet infrastructure "go haywire, after a decent interval, to reset pump speeds and valve settings to produce pressures far beyond those acceptable to pipeline joints and welds." He even goes on to claim that the result "was the most monumental non-nuclear explosion and fire ever seen from space."

This Cold War incident was one of the earliest displays of what is called a "logic bomb" (a piece of code that will set off malicious functions after some time). Not only that, this event probably was the first instance of a full-fledged cyberwar involving moves and countermoves from both parties. Thirty years later, countries and businesses are even more vulnerable. Today, many more important computer systems are connected to the Internet, or at least to some internal network. Nowadays it is not impossible for a terrorist group to turn off the electricity of a whole country by implanting logic bombs. Hackers can cause terrible financial chaos by intruding on Wall Street's automated trading systems or on the security wall of banks' online vaults. More alarmingly, given the fact that computer chips as well as hardware are often made abroad, computer bugs potentially may be planted everywhere, from cutting-edge military equipment to research laboratories. The destructive potential is high enough to scare any defence expert to death.

Since the introductory 1982 incident, cyberspace has strongly emerged as the new fifth domain of warfare, following land, sea, air and space. Many experts believe that, given the overwhelming exposure of modern-day systems to vulnerable networks, a sudden instantaneous failure of computer infrastructure is almost a certainty. According to this school of opinion, collapse of computer networks will, in turn, result in non-functioning factories, exploding chemical plants, satellites spinning out of control and a massive failure of essential infrastructure such as banking and electric power. While this scale of upset seems alarmist to some experts, most agree that the world's tangled and intertwined networks would be pretty easily attacked by those who have the resources, will and time to invest. Many governments know this from their own experience, while some have been easy prey in the hands of skilled hackers; others have employed spies to frequently break into systems and databases, whether Google or defence contractors or anyone else of interest. Unfortunately, penetrating and damaging networks is not much harder. And, unless the perpetrator is miserably careless, no one can prove who did it.

In the last ten years or so, quite a few parties, from government to business corporations, have experienced cyber attacks. Looking back at those incidents can help us learn a lot of things about what went wrong and how things were put right (in the cases in which it was possible). Irrespective of the scale on which they occurred, each holds the key lessons of cyberwar, and it would be alarmingly foolish not to take note of them.

Moonlight Maze and Titan Rain: Birth of a Monster

Moonlight Maze is the popular name of highly classified information-theft attacks on the computer systems at important United States agencies such as NASA, the Pentagon and the Department of Energy and at research labs and private universities. These attacks started in March of 1998 and continued for almost two years without detection. Only late in 2000 did United States officials make note of a patterned probing of computer systems. In what appeared at the time to be the most extensive cyber attack ever aimed at the United States government, covert hackers had systematically broken into Department of Defence computers for more than a year and plundered vast amounts of sensitive information. Besides penetrating the Pentagon's defences, the cyber thieves raided unclassified computer networks at Department of Energy's nuclear weapons and research labs, at the National Aeronautics and Space Administration (NASA), and at numerous university research facilities and defence contractors. Insiders claimed that the intruders were systematically sifting through millions of text and data files, including the maps of military facilities, designs of military equipment and troop configurations. The Department of Defence identified a network of computers in the former U.S.S.R. as the origin of the attack, but obviously, Russia didn't accept any responsibility.

A few years later, in 2003, something similar happened. This time the United States government discovered a series of coordinated attacks on computers that held classified information. Security experts believed that the attacks were Chinese in origin, but any precise details (i.e., whether the incidents constituted corporate espionage, random attacks by individuals or state-sponsored cyberwar) or their real nature (i.e., whether they were carried out by zombie or spyware/virus-infected computers or masked by proxy) remains unknown. In December of 2005, the director of SANS Institute (a reputed security organisation) claimed that the attacks were "most likely the result of Chinese military hackers attempting to gather information on U.S. systems." It is widely believed that the attackers managed to gain access to a number of computer networks in the United States, including those at public and private organisations such as NASA, Lockheed Martin, Redstone Arsenal and Sandia National Laboratories. This attack became popularly known as the Titan's Rain.

These two cyber attacks were much more like secret espionage than an open war, but they did enough to push the alert button. These attacks showed the world for the very first time that, however convenient, the data on our computer systems were not secure. In the past, secret agents had to expend quite some effort to steal a glance at secret defence, space or business documents. Now, they could be downloaded in next to no time, even when the victim was clueless that something was going wrong. These attacks were quite benign in their technical complexity and hence could be neutralized soon after detection. The greater effect was that they left the big guns with the impression that proper cyberwar might not be a far-fetched possibility anymore.

Estonia Cyber Attack: The First Outburst

When it comes to real cyberwar, very few people on this planet have more first-hand experience than JaakAaviksoo. He was Estonia's defence minister in April 2007, when the country's Internet and information systems were interfered with by numerous waves of distributed denial-of-service (DDoS) attacks that knocked several services offline. Estonia, a small country in northern Europe that is heavily dependent on modern networking technologies, is heavily wired: 90 percent of its financial transactions are done electronically, and 70 percent of taxpayers file their returns on the Internet. The Estonian cyber-attacks therefore widely affected the lives of 1.3 million citizens.

Estonia is widely considered one of the most tech-savvy countries in the European Union. As one of the most wired societies in Europe (if not the world) and a pioneer in developing e-governance, Estonia (which declared Internet access a basic human right in 2000) has become dependent on the Internet in every facet of daily life. Even its parliamentary elections take place online. While the country got due applause for being a technology leader, few realised that its overdependence on computers makes it extremely vulnerable to cyber attacks. In 2007, it got a lot of international attention, especially from cyber experts, thanks to a wave of cyber attacks believed to have originated with the Russians, which took place over the course of three weeks. This first known DDos assault, which took cyber attacks from the realm of espionage into the category of true warfare, caused such alarm that NATO began taking apart the incident and studying its implications for the Western alliance.

By way of background, at the start of 2007 Estonia's removal of a Soviet war memorial (the *Bronze Soldier*) in central Tallinn drew Russia into a heated dispute, the two countries' worst since the collapse of the Soviet Union. The barrage of cyber attacks that followed, starting on 27 April, left the websites of government ministries, companies, newspapers, banks and even political parties severely stricken. Attackers ranged from individuals using cheap and simple methods ranging from ping floods to costly implementations of robust botnets, chiefly used to distribute spam. Major news portals commentating on Estonia-Russia tensions and the website of the Estonian Reform Party experienced defacement.

The main targets were the websites of:

- the Estonian presidency and its parliament
- political parties
- almost all of the country's government ministries
- two of the country's biggest banks
- firms specializing in communications
- three of the country's six big news organisations.

A considerable proportion of the attacks targeted large financial institutions, including Swedbank (then known as Hansapank) and SEB. By then, banks were already used to being targeted for all kinds of cybercrimes, so Estonia's banks, compared to government institutions, were well prepared to fend off the attacks. At the peak of the attacks on May 15, hackers managed to stall the SEB website for half an hour. Hansapank's website did not crash, but it faced steep costs in the post-attack period that were reported as no less than EUR 10 million (approximately EEK 156 million).

The attacks came in three waves: 1) from 27 April (the day when the *Bronze Soldier* riots started), peaking around 3 May; 2) and 8 and 9 May (two of the most celebrated dates in the Russian calendar, when the country observes Victory Day over Nazi Germany); and 3) the third week of May. The attacks poured in from all over the world, but computer security experts, as well as Estonian officials, claimed that some attackers, particularly in the initial phases, were traced by their Internet (IP) addresses—most of which were Russian. Some attackers even appeared to be from Russian state institutions. A few online communities also allegedly revealed the Russian origin of these attacks.

Estonian officials claimed that one of the masterminds was identified by his online nickname being connected to the Russian security service. Later, a nineteen-year-old college student was arrested in Tallinn for his alleged involvement.

Experts said that the attacks were not extremely sophisticated. The attackers mostly used techniques that had been in existence for quite some time, but the focus of the attacks was to completely shut down the information technology infrastructure of the country. The waves of distributed denial-of-Service (DDoS) attacks launched against websites saw them suddenly overwhelmed by millions of visits. This jammed and disabled them by swamping the bandwidths of the servers on which the sites ran. The attackers used botnet attacks to launch a DDoS rendering system that rendered the Internet useless. (A botnet is a hijacked computer that sends out huge amounts of information to swamp an Internet server. The increased traffic causes a site's host server to exceed its bandwidth capability and results in a shutdown.)

One U.S. Embassy report quoted Rein Ottis, the head of cyber defence at the Estonian Defence Ministry, as saying that the attacks against key Internet routers and servers in Estonia could potentially knock down the country's whole infrastructure. A more neutral assessment suggests that Estonian Internet access was never under such serious threat, even at the peak of the attacks. Based on the technological prowess they had, the Estonians responded to the cyber attacks very proficiently. They were able to coordinate responses that secured only relatively short-term outages instead of any permanent damage to the country's IT infrastructure. The Estonian government was quick to employ its cyber counterespionage group, the Computer Emergency Response Team (CERT), which coordinated IT responses among civilian and government specialists. HillarAarelaid, chief security officer of CERT, was famously quoted as saying, "Yes, it's a serious problem, but we are up and running." And indeed, even the most affected websites resumed service within a month.

Estonia managed to get away with only modest damage from the attacks, mainly because of its small size. As a result of its size, the Internet security experts of various institutions knew each other closely and formed an effective informal network to cooperate against the attacks. The Estonian observers who kept an eye on the Russian hackers' web forums also provided some useful intelligence data. Due to the inexact nature of the Internet as a communications medium, however, Estonians were unable to decisively prove the identity of the attackers. Most hid securely behind veils of fake Internet Protocol (IP) addresses, but these could not stop widespread speculation about Russian involvement.

The botnet attacks on the Estonian IT systems ended as abruptly as they started. This obviously strengthens the leading Estonian officials' allegation that the attacks were part of planned and coordinated warfare. (As a matter of fact, Botnets can be installed on any computer at any place well in advance of a planned attack. Unless computer administrators have installed proper protective software on the affected computers, they may never even know that their machines have been hijacked and are being used in a cyber attack. If we keep this in mind, the Estonian cyber attacks actually demonstrate the vulnerability of IT systems that depend on the Internet. The use of technology definitely can improve personal and business as well as government communications, but it is still extremely vulnerable to interruptions and attacks. The lessons from Estonia were summarized very well by Defence Minister Aaviksoo: "Extensive cyber-attacks against Estonia show clearly that this matter should be seriously dealt with and relevant information exchanged with one another."

Middle-East Mayhem

Israel and Lebanon were facing a lot of turmoil in 2006 as death tolls on both sides of their conflict were on the rise. And then, suddenly, the conflict exploded onto the Internet frontier as groups of computer hackers unleashed a series of severe cyber attacks on thousands of Western and Israeli websites. According to Roberto Preatoni, founder of the crime observatory website www.zone-h.org, this was the largest- ever politically motivated cyber attack. This mass war against a national enemy was the Battle of Stalingrad of the cyber era. More than ten thousand websites reportedly found themselves caught in this crossfire. Attacks flooded everyone, everywhere: from businesses to government agencies to military services, no one was spared. At its peak, four thousand websites were attacked each day. More than 80 percent of these attacks drew inspiration from the escalating conflict between Hezbollah and Israel. An overwhelming majority of the attacks were directed against American, European and, of course, Israeli websites. One minute these websites were benign vendors auctioning electronic items or public-service sites detailing government norms. The very next minute, the sites were torn apart and replaced by digital emblems of protest: burning words and images demanding an end to the war.

Until this attack, cyberwars had targeted the websites of bigger institutions including military bases, banks and research organisations in limited numbers. Now, thousands of small- and medium-size business websites (often easy prey for an attacker) as well as a large number of heavily secured sites had been downed. The attackers got clearer with their purpose and replaced the immaculate web business pages with bloodstained images of wounded children and gun-toting soldiers bursting into homes.

This new trend raised quite a few eyebrows in apprehension. The escalating attack volume was certainly worrying. For the time being, protesters were satisfied with making their points with images and words, but had they chosen a more aggressive approach, the results surely could have been very devastating. For example, if hackers had unleashed a series of DDoS attacks to rip down major sites such as Haaretz (an Israeli news organisation) or eBay, the consequence could have been a truly disturbing outage.

As the Middle East attacks were not DDoS or botnet attacks, the damage was relatively easy to fix. Most of the defaced websites were quick to remove the infected pages, and on a positive note, most took the matter quite seriously and made efforts to plug their security holes.

In last two years, the Middle East and North Africa both have been very active politically. A lot of questions are being raised about the people in power, especially regarding freedom of speech and democratic rights for ordinary people. At the same time, there is general rage against Western countries, which are frequently viewed by the locals as imperialist oppressors. This has given rise to a new war scenario in cyberspace: The Internet has turned into a major battlefield for activists. Some of the protesters are using the Internet as an extremely effective channel through which to communicate, train and spread the ideologies of aggressive nationalism—basically using the Internet as an advanced media channel. On the other hand, more aggressive activists are using DDoS and other attack techniques to disrupt any "web peace" that may have seemed to exist in Western cyberspace (effectively no less than 70 percent of the whole).

Hacking is much easier to execute than a gun assault—and more often than not, taking down a website means much more far-reaching destruction than killing a soldier. This hacking as activism—or "Hacktivism," as practitioners call it—is spreading like a cyber worm.

Hacktivism, a word compiled from *hacking* and *activism,* is used to describe cyber attacks as a part of a larger activist propaganda campaign and is a classic example of politics meeting technology—and creating havoc. A number of anonymous groups working from Tunisia, Egypt, Libya, Algeria and other Middle East/North African countries are increasingly engaged in hacktivist activities. Hacktivists work on a number of issues: warfare against the websites of the "enemies," providing support to bypass the ruling regimes' censorship of the Internet, bringing down web-based services, spreading the word about their ideology, activities and advice.

The situation is somewhat different when it comes to website defacement, an important component of Hacktivism. The evidence at Zone-H's website-defacement archive is that the number of such acts due to political reasons has escalated rapidly in 2010, and that a lot of defacement attacks originate in the Middle East. A lot of people are trying their hands at it, even if they do not really care about hacktivism. Intentions vary widely; websites are being defaced for politics, propaganda, financial gain, ego, thrill and even fun. From skilled hackers to "script kiddies" (tech geek slang to describe anyone who copies scripts for hacking), everyone is working for the same. This makes the whole scenario even more chaotic and tough to control, as it's difficult to check random attackers who hardly follow a pattern.

One of the latest hacktivist assaults was executed against the Voice of America's website. As more protests unfold in the Middle East, the overseer of U.S. international broadcasting says its outlets serving that area face increased satellite signal interference as well as a web Domain Name System attack. On 21 February 2011, officials of the Broadcasting Board of Governors (BBG), responsible for non-military international broadcasts out of the United States, reported that unknown attackers had hacked www.voanews.com, the primary domain name of Voice of America. The attackers also defaced a bunch of other websites registered with domain-name marketer Network Solutions. All of the users were automatically directed to a website that claimed to be run by the Iranian Cyber Army. BBG saw this as another assault on free media and strongly condemned it without any tangible result, since the number of defaced sites continues to rise.

Operation Aurora: The First Direct Attack on a Corporate

On 12 January 2010, Google came out with an explosive entry on its official blog. For the first time it publicly admitted that its corporate infrastructure has been targeted in a very sophisticated attack, which the company claimed had originated from China. According to Google, the aim of this attack was to access the email accounts of Chinese human-rights activists. Both Google and China have spoken out about this issue, causing a rift in the once lucrative business venture. Google rerouted their servers through Hong Kong, which caused a loss in profit when Chinese search engines (most notably Baidu)moved in to fill the gap.

On 12 June 2011, CBS reported a second infiltration of Google, originating from a Chinese city with a major military base. It is widely believed that these are covert operations intended to collect intelligence on the US government. China states that these accusations are false. Today, whenever Google speaks out about the censorship and hacking, it reports trouble with servers. The Chinese government denies any interference, claiming to also be harmed by the incidents.

Adobe Systems, Rackspace and Juniper Networks also confirmed such attacks soon after Google. According to media reports, a number of other companies including Dow Chemical, Morgan Stanley, Symantec and Yahoo also were attacked. According to Dmitri Alperovitch (Vice President of Threat Research at McAfee, the famous computer security firm), the goal of these attacks was to gain access to and modify source code repositories at important high-tech security and defence contractor companies.

Later on, McAfee labelled this attack Operation Aurora, after part of the file path on the attacker's machine that was included in two crimeware binaries confirmed to have been associated with this attack. The coordinated Aurora assault exploited a vulnerability in Microsoft Internet Explorer to gain access to a user's computer. These attacks were secretly launched whenever target users visited a malicious web page that looked innocuously similar to trustworthy websites. Thereafter, malware was automatically downloaded and activated within the system, creating a connection between the attacked computer and a remote server. This connection was used to steal intellectual properties from the companies or the account details of targeted email accounts. The attacks were noted for their sophistication and complexity. The attackers used multiple layers of encryption and took unprecedented precautions to avoid detection.

The Chinese government was widely viewed as the force behind Aurora. Reports have quoted a diplomatic cable from the U.S. Embassy in Beijing suggesting that the attacks were part of a campaign carried out by "government operatives, public security experts and Internet outlaws recruited by the Chinese government." The report also claimed that this operation was part of a bigger ongoing campaign in which hackers have "broken into American government computers and those of Western allies, the Dalai Lama and American businesses since 2002."

Implications for Businesses

Many experts who analysed the Aurora operation have claimed that the attack was a well-coordinated assault on the intellectual properties of major corporate houses. Operation Aurora has clearly shown that major companies across sectors are extremely lucrative as targets of web attacks. Many high-profile corporates are extremely vulnerable to targeted attacks that exploit the zero-day vulnerabilities (i.e. the vulnerabilities that are still unknown to the software developers) of some software (e.g., browsers, operating systems, etc.) used by the companies. If an attacker is skilled enough, highly valuable loot— the intellectual property of major firms, which basically translates to their business advantage— is there for his taking. Like an army of cheats withdrawing money from an ATM, installed malware enabled the hackers to quietly take out the corporates' crown jewels while their executives were enjoying their December holidays. Aurora showed that it was high time for corporates to realise that they cannot keep every business secret on their computer hard discs without taking extreme caution about their security.

Cyber Terrorism

A group of unknowns, appropriately named Anonymous, are the most watched cyber terrorist at this time. They attack systems not for information, but to terrorize and attempt to strong-hold companies or countries into following demands. The group, purportedly with no leader, came together in 2003 from the website imageboard 4chan. Although their original intent was to cause mayhem for fun, they quickly started using cyber attacks in an attempt to have demands met.

Anonymous were made famous in 2008 when they began their cyber attack on the Church of Scientology. The Church had attempted to remove, from a website, a video of Tom Cruise speaking to the parishioners. Anonymous demanded that the Church be removed from the internet. Through the prodding of an ex-Scientology member, their attacks quickly shifted to peaceful protests.

This wasn't the end of the groups' terrorist acts, however. On the night of 15 June, 2011, Anonymous bombarded Malaysian Government Websites. The attack was spurred by the fact that Maylasia censured Wikileaks (Anonymous is believed to be a contributor to the site). Despite having plenty of warning from a threat issued by Anonymous, the government lost access for several hours to 41 websites; 51 were affected altogether.

Anonymous set their sights to other governments, including the United States, Australia, Zimbabwe and Tunisia. In response to this, governments are actively attempting to locate anyone participating in such attacks. In January 2011, the United States FBI has issued search warrants and stated that the offence can lead to up to 10 years in prison. The British, Australian and Turkish Governments have arrested suspects in conjunction with Anonymous. Datuk Fadillah Yusuf, Deputy Minister of Science, Technology and Innovation for Malaysia, has taken the attacks as proof that cyberwar is a viable threat. He addressed the attackers, suggesting that they not forget the people of Malaysia who were caught in the middle of the terrorist act.

Government Response

As a response to Cyber attacks, the Prime Minister of Malaysia created IMPACT Global Headquarters on 20th May 2009. It is comprised of 136 countries and focuses on fighting threats and attacks. Impact offers training courses to help countries and businesses protect themselves. Some courses are Computer Forensics Analysis, Malware Analysis and Reverse Engeneerinig, which speaks to the world's full immersion into the fifth domain of warfare.

Europe has created a Task Force to deal with cyber threats, also. As of 2011, the European Electronic Crime Task Force (EECTF) has analyzed cybercrimes in 2010 and they also look at the legal issues that may arise. In the 2011 EECTF Survey, created to study specifically the effects of cybercrime in Europe, EECTF states, "Given the global nature of the cyberthreat, the task force intends to play a leading role, at both European and international level..." A majority of Governments are beginning to realize that cybercrime is a serious issue that requires serious attention.

In the past, the DoD had commented on how difficult drawing up war plans for cyber threats is due to a lack of maps and terrains. On 14 July, 2011, the DoD released news about a new strategy. These plans came after 24,000 files were taken in March 2011. Not much was stated about the files or the military contractor they purportedly belonged to. With the continued threat, the DoD has created a preliminary defence plan. The plan consists of training military in cyberspace, using new defence options, collaborating within the government and with allies, and utilizing the latest in US technology. After the preliminary defence plan, they will implement a second plan, which includes creating a healthier system, monitor for inside threats, and restructuring networks. While the plan does not include specifics (as many assumed it would not), this shows how the government has had to work in order to protect its systems, as should all businesses.

Two Mighty Blows

But the worst was yet to come. And when it actually came, it left all the traditional cyber security measures in mayhem. For a long time no one knew what to do; security experts didn't know how to react, the big-house software firms were hovering over the newly exploited vulnerabilities, and affected corporates were already on their knees.

The attacks described in the last chapter were certainly severe. For the most part, though, they were not severe enough (except, in a few instances, for Operation Aurora) to generate huge public and media buzz. These attacks came and went away, but very few, other than those affected, paid attention. Cyberwar still was something perceived as relatively benign, hardly something that could shake the foundations of our societies and civilisation as traditional war does. This view soon changed, however, mainly because of two attacks that attracted as much media and public attention as any natural disaster. Both shook up traditional ideas about cyber security and demonstrated the vulnerability of all corporate communications, systems and databases. One of them was WikiLeaks, the notoriously famous (or infamous, according to some) whistle blower website that made all the major U.S. corporates worry about one question: "What if we are next?" The other earth-shaking attack, called Stuxnet, became equally famous by virtually stopping the operations of infected industries. Stuxnet demonstrated the vulnerability of the industrial software that today is heavily used across different sectors.

WikiLeaks: The Future of Cyberwar?

A certain Julian Assange and his non-profit venture WikiLeaks were unheard of even five years ago. In 2010 and into 2011, however, they have created nothing short of the most talked-about media havoc of the digital-news era. After working as a whistle blower for quite some time on a wide range of issues from Kenya to Peru and Somalia to the United States, WikiLeaks, in 2010, shook international politics to its foundations by publishing thousands of secret cables dispatched by U.S. diplomats over a considerable period of time. While WikiLeaks' founder has been worshipped as a hero by many free-speech and pro-media groups, the organisation also has faced heavy criticism in U.S. diplomatic circles for harming national security and compromising international diplomacy.

In the midst of the political mayhem, very few people have noticed another significant implication of the WikiLeaks affair. Although everyone seems to be very worried about the political issues, not many have taken a note of WikiLeaks' effect on business secrets. WikiLeaks clearly demonstrated how the cosy comfort of Internet convenience can be infiltrated to extract all the secrets you have ever had. The most alarming fact is that you won't even realise this disaster has happened unless the culprits feel like telling you. While whistle blowers may toot their horns in public, corporate competitors will hardly do so; they would rather reap the fruits of their special knowledge to counter their victims' business strategies. The victim in turn will hardly realise why their carefully honed strategies are not working. This frightening thought is reason enough to explore how WikiLeaks' espionage was executed, how similar things can happen to business corporations and how potential corporate victims could possibly counter them.

The Doers and the Deeds

WikiLeaks, launched in 2006 under an organisation named The Sunshine Press, is a website that publishes the confidential documents of governments, businesses and other powerful organisations, often received from anonymous sources (with some exceptions, such as when real whistle blowers happen to step forward). WikiLeaks takes pride in calling itself an "uncensorable version of Wikipedia," and claims to share the ideologies, processes and designs of the renowned online encyclopaedia. These two websites, however, have no formal relationship. The WikiLeaks website describes Assange, its Australian founder, as "Australia's most famous ethical computer hacker." Unnamed journalists, mathematicians, Chinese dissidents and some technology-minded people are also credited with its creation.

When it comes to uncovering secrets, WikiLeaks certainly spares no one. The Church of Scientology, Hollywood celebrities, the US military, the Kenyan police and even wealthy Swiss banks all have had to endure embarrassing WikiLeaks disclosures in the recent past.

How WikiLeaks Works

WikiLeaks' operations are always kept under the wrap of extreme secrecy. By intention, the site does not operate from any headquarters. Experts believe that WikiLeaks is operated by five individual "investigators" who assess and verify the genuineness of submitted documents. The verified documents are believed to be uploaded to servers in Sweden and then "mirrored" by a number of servers across the globe. This decentralized organisational structure makes shutting WikiLeaks down particularly difficult.

At one stage, WikiLeaks claimed that it had broken through the encryptions of the American military in order to access the video it posted of the United States air force shooting Iraqi civilians and journalists. Whether the group obtained an encrypted video from a third-party or actually hacked through the Department of Defence's firewalls to gain access to the footage remains unclear.

In the case of secret cables on the Iraq and Afghanistan wars, they received assistance from a rogue U.S. army private named Bradley Manning. Experts have attempted to unearth how Bradley Manning managed to access those highly secret cables in such large volumes. It has been noted that the United States military had recently launched an initiative named Net-Centric Diplomacy to increase information sharing among offices and employees. Under this fresh initiative, a significant number of State Department documents were made available through a SIPNET (Secret Internet Protocol Router Network), which was supposed to be the Pentagon's secure and secret global network. Any information published on this network was to be accessible only to authorized U.S. military-service personnel. While the SIPNET did ease sharing of information among a select group of people, its basis in good faith exposed a huge amount of classified information to the risk of betrayal. In the end, Manning simply downloaded a large number of documents available to him on the SIPNET and passed them on to WikiLeaks.

The thought of a Wikileaks attack is especially worrisome because of the group's two-pronged operations strategy. Their hackers, as good as anyone who has ever worked this business, can not only make their way through all of the security mazes of a corporation (remember how they recently attacked the websites of a few major financial institutions who suspended WikiLeaks' accounts), but can also mask their footprints very well, making it impossible to ever find them or retrieve lost information. The talented staff hackers, who regularly contribute contents to WikiLeaks, continuously probe and gain access to important websites, from which they download information. At the same time, they also have many well-placed sources ready to compromise stacks of information for some reason or other.

Implications for Businesses: Why Worry?

Big corporates always have been concerned about Internet privacy, especially since the birth of corporate espionage. Top executives generally don't share their classified information over vulnerable email services or leave their work computers unprotected, but the risks to privacy are now much graver than the occasional leak of executive mail to public media. The real threat is that companies' corporate brains will be exposed, just as the United States' government's "diplomatic brain" has been opened in front of all. Very few things can cause greater worry for the public relations departments of victimized firms. Since public reputation affects sales and revenue, a threat to reputation is a threat to business operations and, of course, profitability. Bank of America's stock dropped 3 percent in a single trading day just on the rumour that WikiLeaks had the company in its sights. Reputations have bottom-line impact, and in a world where leaking and publishing private documents is increasingly easy, reputations are all the more vulnerable.

Until now, firms have been able to find ways to survive. Remember the case of Goldman Sachs, the large U. S. investment bank suspected of causing the current global recession? Early in 2010, Goldman Sachs gave literally terabytes of data on government officials looking for the irregularities that could have caused the financial crisis. All of the bankers desperately looking to avoid government regulations cheered the sheer brilliance of Goldman's manoeuvre; with limited time and computational resources, finding anything meaningful in that heap of data was practically impossible for investigators. The result, however, could have been much different if all of that data had found its way onto the WikiLeaks website. Casual visitors to WikiLeaks, like government investigators with limited resources and time, could not possibly find anything of interest before running out of patience. A competitor, however, would surely expend much more effort (and have greater skill) in extracting useful information from the heap. Aggressive hedge funds, in particular, which employ armies of skilled programmers to search out anything that could provide an edge in the market, might spend a whole day or two searching for signs of weakness or any pointers to upcoming happenings.

Such a scenario is certainly not just a thought experiment or stretch of the imagination. WikiLeaks has promised a significant information dump on a large financial institution in 2011. In an interview with *Forbes* magazine, Julian Assange declared that at least half of the treasure trove of documents his organisation is sitting on belongs to private corporations, and that sometime early in 2011, it plans a megadump of materials belonging to one of the United States' leading banks. For many years, cyber-security experts have warned of the significant threat from disgruntled insiders who have full access to databases with confidential information guarded only by poorly crafted security policies. Nothing in WikiLeaks' victims' list suggests that the group cannot or will not use its skills to reveal the embarrassing secrets of powerful corporations.

What if the company you work for has nothing to hide? What if yours is an extremely transparent organisation with no need to hold back any fact or mask any move?

First, such an ideal is almost impossible in today's world. Very few businesses will be eager to share their trade secrets and strategic decisions in a competitive environment, so there's no such thing as utter transparency. Second, even if a company is not exposed directly, it could be caught in a tug-of-war between government and whistle blowers. Particularly if your company is perceived as pro-government, it runs a high risk of attack from thousands of unknown hackers who are extremely capable of at least dislodging all of a company's web-based services. This is exactly what happened to many leading financial-services firms (especially the ones with transaction businesses such as credit cards).

Responses to WikiLeaks: How to Survive the Blows

Any corporation, just like a U.S. military, has to allow authorised personnel some access to classified data if it wants to put that data to any use. Generally, this is managed by trying to take sufficient care in choosing who will be authorized for access. But the WikiLeaks incident certainly shows that this procedure is not foolproof in the presence of an authorised insider with unsuspected motives. Tightening the authorisation process is obviously a very important step to be taken to ensure that only extremely reliable people gain access to secret information. Businesses can learn from the immediate steps the U.S. military took in reaction to the WikiLeaks incident.

On August 12, 2010, two review committees commissioned by Robert Gates, Secretary of Defence for the United States, undertook the task of determining the technological, procedural and policy shortfalls that could have contributed to the embarrassing disclosures to WikiLeaks. As per their reports, the military presented a number of findings and recommendations. The most important of these are:

- Action was taken to disable all write capability from classified military computers, as a temporary technical solution to prevent authorised employees from moving secret information to external systems such as removable drives and storage devices.
- Defence organisations were asked to authorize only a few systems through which to move data from classified systems to unclassified systems.
- Defence organisations implemented new "two-person handling rules" for moving data to outside computers. Now any data that has to be moved out of a classified system will require checking by at least two personnel. This rule is expected to ensure proper attention to intentions and reduce the chances of unauthorised release of secret information by a single employee.
- As a technical response to the leaks, which exploited the weaknesses of SIPR systems, 60 percent of Defence's SIPR network has been equipped with a Host Based Security System (HBBS), an automated control procedure with the ability to monitor unusual data usage or access to the computer system. This is expected to help in detecting and monitoring suspicious or unusual user behaviour. This process is similar to the data-analysis-based procedures used by credit card firms to curb fraud cases.

These responses to the WikiLeaks crisis are expected to make it much more difficult for a determined actor to get access to and move information outside of authorized channels.

A more novel approach to counter leaks could be what experts are calling "information masking." It works exactly the way a secure system disguises a password, by converting every bit of it into code, jumbling up the sequences or changing every bit following a known pattern. The whole conversion has to be done in a specific algorithm, so that the "code" can again be decoded when the information is needed. This makes the process of information transfer much safer and more secure, but at the price of being cumbersome. Since advanced cryptographic methods are used for this purpose, a business must have skilled cryptographers and programmers on board in order to execute something of this complexity. An alternative could be employing a professional cryptography research firm, but depending upon the secrecy involved in a business, giving outsiders a peek might not be wise.

To-Dos to Prevent Leaks: Prepare, Prepare and Prepare

Identifying the risks of leakage should be the first step in prevention. Do employees talk about corporate secrets casually on your firm's internal emails? Do managers describe in unpleasing terms how the company plans to take on competitors or exploit its customers? To put it simply, would the company's internal emails cause embarrassment if leaked to public media? If the answer is Yes, a company has no option but to develop a logical argument to explain that "embarrassing" behaviour, not only to the public but also to all the stakeholders, should be avoided. To ensure long-term risk-free internal communication, corporate culture may need thorough re-examination, so that employee behaviour becomes aligned with the desired public image. What happens in Vegas (or in this case, in in-house emails) does not stay in Vegas any more, but ends up finding its way to WikiLeaks, leading to unanticipated debacles. Businesses that really want to stay safe should start working on a more transparent internal corporate culture with high employee morale.

Historically, data-security concerns in businesses have been focused on external threats, whether from hackers or from corporate espionage. The lesson from WikiLeaks shows that the documents that end up getting published don't have to be stolen by outsiders. A number of unhappy insiders can also provide whistle blowers with classified information. Most WikiLeaks "sources" are none other than company personnel. Reasonably happy employees normally won't leak documents, so companies should periodically assess the sentiment and satisfaction of their employees, making sincere efforts to address points of concern, especially any psychological blocks.

Of course, having tight digital security and strict information norms won't do any harm. It's very important to keep possible hackers at bay by tightening the security measures of your websites, firewalls, internal email or virtually any digital information that you consider classified.

The prominence of WikiLeaks is forcing businesses (and, of course, national administrations) to think, What if we're next? Preparing for the worst is always good, ensuring that a company has a structured risk assessment, scenario planning and developing action plans, just like any other body in charge of disaster management. Disaster management certainly deserves regard as an important operational function, not just an afterthought left to the public relations department. In short, proactive management is called for to handle this new leakage risk.

While WikiLeaks may have taught corporates a thing or two about maintaining secrecy, most probably felt that their business processes looked pretty solid and secure. Factories were running automatically by virtue of industrial software (e.g., SCADA systems), and there was little reason to think that these automations could be disrupted by security concerns—until, that is, Stuxnet emerged into the corporate wilds and put everyone into a frenzy.

Stuxnet: Father of Targeted Malware

Targeted industrial malware was not widely known until the dreadful outburst of Stuxnet in early 2010. On the face of it, Stuxnet may look like just any other malware, but as a matter of fact, it might be the pioneering exploit of a whole new breed. The Stuxnet infection has turned out to be of supreme relevance for the business processes of today.

SCADA Systems: Backbone of Infrastructure, Facilities and Industrial Processes

Supervisory Control and Data Acquisition systems, more popularly known as SCADAs, is a family of industrial-control systems: computer systems that monitor and control industrial (e.g. production, manufacturing, fabrication, power generation, refining, etc.), infrastructure (e.g., oil and gas pipelines, wastewater treatment and collection, electrical-power generation and distribution, wind firms, etc.) or facility-based processes (e.g., systems governing all the processes in private and public facilities such as buildings, airports, ships, space stations, etc.). More often than not, a SCADA system co-ordinates but does not control processes in real time. Public as well as private businesses rely heavily on them. Real-time control is considered to be the forte of the newer telecommunications technologies, which enable reliable, high-speed, low-latency communications over wide areas. Most differences between SCADAs and DCSs (Distributed Control Systems) are culturally determined and are usually not significant, especially from an operations point of view.

In most developed countries, SCADAs basically run everything from the power at home to air conditioning in offices to the whole communication systems. Public as well as private enterprises depend heavily on such systems. If someone can break into the security barriers of SCADA systems, havoc will ensue when the whole operations system of a country or company cripples in either industrial production or day-to-day life—or both.

Why SCADAs Are Vulnerable

The move to standardized and open solutions from the more traditional proprietary technologies—along with the increased number of connections between SCADA systems, the Internet and office networks—has raised quite a few eyebrows in concern. Many experts complain that SCADAs actually make companies even more vulnerable to cyber attacks. As a result, the security of SCADA-based systems has come into question as they are increasingly perceived as extremely vulnerable to cyberwar and cyber terrorism attacks. Unfortunately, most businesses make little effort to ensure the security of such systems. Richard Clark, a revered computer security expert, once commented that industries spend more on coffee than on systems securities—and his comment can hardly be seen as unjustified.

The major issues cited as the reasons for SCADAs' vulnerability are as follows:

1. These systems are supposed to run automatically for years, if not for ages. Obviously, they don't need authentication or, more popularly speaking, login. Without a provision for regular password change to keep a system robust, the identity of an automated system faces a huge set of problems that may result in unwanted automated access to high-security systems.
2. Since the authentication process is absent in the network, restricting someone in the network from accessing any part of it is practically impossible. This makes the whole system dangerously tangled and easy to attack.
3. A lot of old SCADA systems still in use (especially in developing countries) do not have any options for security patching. After installation, such systems run as is for no less than five years. Given the way new security threats are evolving with each passing day, protecting a five- year-old system that does not include any up-to-date security features is virtually impossible.
4. Current SCADA systems have a high degree of exposure to external networks such as the Internet and private office networks.

History and Experts' Reactions

Stuxnet was the first crimeware used with the specific purpose of attacking industrial control system networks. This malware was first reported in June of 2010 by a Belarusian computer security firm named VirusBlokAda. Initially, cyber-security researchers thought that this virus started spreading in March or April of 2010. Later on, it emerged that the first variant of this worm had started infecting systems almost a year previously, in June 2009. A second version hit in April 2010 and had various vital improvements, reportedly because the authors thought that the virus was spreading rather slowly. (Note that the attackers constantly monitored their handiwork and were in a position to change their script to make the worm more threatening.) A slightly modified third version surfaced a month later.

Stuxnet created brouhaha among cyber-security experts. Kaspersky Labs, one of the foremost security-service vendors, released a statement saying, "Stuxnet is a working and fearsome prototype of a cyber-weapon that will lead to the creation of a new arms race in the world." In a report published in *Vanity Fair* magazine in April 2011, Michael Gross termed Stuxnet "the Hiroshima of cyberwar." Government cyber-security experts from the United States have described Stuxnet as "a precision, military-grade cyber missile deployed early last year to seek out and destroy one real-world target of high importance." What made Stuxnet markedly different from all of its peers was its high degree of complexity. This piece of malware was much bigger and more complex than all other threats seen to date; the Conficker Worm, the previous heavyweight malware champion, was only one-twentieth of Stuxnet's size. Roel Schouwenberg, a senior expert at Kaspersky Labs, called Stuxnet's deployment "groundbreaking." According to Schouwenberg, Stuxnet made other cyber attacks, including the much talked-about Operation Aurora, look like child's play.

Most researchers believe that Stuxnet required huge support in terms of finance, resources and intelligence. To quote Liam OMurchu, an operations manager at Symantec's security-response group, "It's amazing, really, the resources that went into this worm." Ralph Langner, chief of a security firm that deals exclusively with industrial control systems, was the first analyst to reverse-engineer Stuxnet's payload. In an interview with the *Christian Science Monitor*, he stated that the preparation for this highly sophisticated malware must have involved a team composed of "intel, covert ops, exploit writers, process engineers, control system engineers, product specialists, and military liaison." This high-resource component of Stuxnet gives rise to speculation that it was a state-backed attack, since few entities could afford to fund something so big.

How Does Stuxnet Work and Spread?

The complex Stuxnet malware targeted attacks against three different computer systems used widely in industry: PLCs (programmable logic controllers) by Siemens, the Windows operating systems by Microsoft and Step 7 industrial software running on Microsoft Windows (e.g., Siemens' WinCC/PCS 7 SCADA control software). In short, the Stuxnet worm was capable of altering the PLCs, tiny computing systems about the size of a crayon pack, that form the heart of any industrial system. PLCs control and regulate almost all automated processes in factories, construction projects, airports, power plants, etc. The virus appeared to be capable of taking control of the automated control systems executed by the infected PLCs, doing with them whatever the attacker programmed it to do. Potentially, Stuxnet could stall large chunks of the industrial processes at infected sites.

Stuxnet exploited many of the in-built vulnerabilities in the Windows operating system. Two were the already exploited CPLINK vulnerability (which allows a shortcut link, known as a .lnk file, to run a harmful DLL script) and another vulnerability previously used by the Conficker malware. In addition to these, Stuxnet executed four zero-day attacks on infected Microsoft Windows systems (a zero-day attack exploits vulnerabilities in software that are unknown to its software developer). Stuxnet's attack was unprecedented and astonishing, since zero-day vulnerabilities in a system as famous and widely used as Microsoft Windows are rare and precious. The feat of investing four such vulnerabilities in a single worm was part of what made Stuxnet markedly deadlier than previous malware attacks. The Stuxnet malware code was especially large—.5 MB to 1.5 MB in size—and was written in various programming languages (including C++ and C). The part that targeted Windows was programmed to spread very fast but in a very innocuous way.

Stuxnet also spread in some novel ways from one system to another. Initially, it spread through infected removable storage devices, such as USB flash drives, which infected other computers whenever they were inserted into another computer. The malware automatically uploaded two files from the USB device into the computer. One of them was a rootkit dropper; an executable (.exe) file that installs a rootkit—a piece of software that enables a remote attacker to gain continued privileged access to a system while hiding its presence from the administrators. A rootkit dropper enables an attacker to do practically anything he wants with a victim's computer. The other automatically installed file was a heavily encrypted payload of malicious scripts. The deadliest feature of Stuxnet is its ability to hide all of its actions and components as soon as it forges its way in. On top of that, Stuxnet was the first malware that actually used a stolen genuine digital signature instead of a forged one like those usually appended to common viruses. The signature employed was somehow stolen from Realtek, one of the most trusted software publishers. This signature caused anti-virus programmes and other maintenance software to recognize Stuxnet as trustworthy (and to fail to recognize it as a virus). Use of the stolen signature was the digital equivalent of a criminal carrying a policeman's genuine ID card. The later versions of Stuxnet exploited other channels such as P2P (peer-to-peer) RPCs (Remote Procedure Calls) to spread infection and update infected computers that were not connected to the Internet.

PLCs and Industrial control systems have certainly been targeted before, but Stuxnet was the first instance of an attack that was remotely programmed to physically alter control systems without any fingers on a keyboard somewhere. Stuxnet looked like a self-directed, self-controlled, intelligent stealth drone: the first known malware that, unleashed into the wild, can find a certain target, sabotage it, and hide both its presence as well as its effects till the damage is complete. This was, and still is, revolutionary by any means.

What Can It Do?

Once Stuxnet finds its way into a computer through the USB ports, it opens a backdoor to the Internet and then contacts a remote host (claimed to be in Denmark or Malaysia) for instructions. For computers not connected to the Internet, Stuxnet collects instructions via local networks (e.g., P2P networks, shared folders, etc.). After receiving instructions, Stuxnet can make complex modifications to PLCs, which virtually allows the attackers to alter key processes as they wish. PLC codes can be modified to stop motors, change the direction of a conveyer belt, stall pumps and effectively stop a whole factory in the blink of an eye. Experts believe Stuxnet's power is such that, if modifications were executed well, this virus could even cause a petroleum refinery or nuclear power plant to explode.

Another Stuxnet specialty is its ability to attack only its targets. Stuxnet looks for a specific configuration of industrial equipment as it spreads infection. An attack is launched only when it finds an exact match. Siemens reported that for no less than fifteen infected plants around the globe, operations remained unaffected as they were not among the intended targets.

Target and Origin

A statement by Symantec on 6 August 2010, claimed that more than 68 percent of Stuxnet-infected systems were in Iran (about 14 percent were in Indonesia, 7 percent in India, 3 percent each in the United States and Australia, and 1 percent each in the United Kingdom, Malaysia and Pakistan). This infection distribution gave rise to speculation that the Stuxnet virus had targeted Iran. Some experts think that the Bushehr nuclear reactor could have been a possible target. Government officials from Iran confirmed that Stuxnet infected systems at Bushehr, but they also said that no heavy damage was done to its major systems. As a matter of fact, Bushehr has been dogged by several issues in the last few years and, given this history, would not appear to have been a very lucrative target for the attackers. A more probable target might have been the uranium-enrichment plant at Natanz. The United Nations—appointed watchdog, the International Atomic Energy Agency, did report that Stuxnet idled almost half of the centrifuges at the plant and even appeared to lower the yield of the working ones. Many experts believe this slowdown was proof of Stuxnet's prowess.

The virus' origin is also much debated. Israel looks like the obvious culprit, with both the motive and technological power to attack the Iranian nuclear programme—a real threat from the Israeli perspective. A few other countries also have the technical capability to execute such an attack, among them China, the United States, Russia and even France and Germany, according to many experts. Some reports have suggested that the United States has a clear motive to sabotage Iran's nuclear reactors, and many believe that Stuxnet was a joint ploy of Israel and the United States. Nothing is known as a certainty, however, and all claims about the origin of Stuxnet are reasonable guesses at best.

Implications for Businesses

Stuxnet presented a whole new threat scenario to businesses that use information technology systems (e.g., automation, databases, PLCs and even the Internet). As an individual worm, Stuxnet was too targeted to create mass panic, but it demonstrated the power of malware that exploits zero-day vulnerabilities. If a competitor targeted a major corporate using a Stuxnet-like virus, the rival could easily slip in one infected drive and infect all of the target's computers. With the computers all infected, the competitor would gain virtual control over each business and production process and shape them to its own ends. The attacker could stop those business processes, shape them to its own benefit or at the very least gain vital knowledge about them. The most threatening part is that an infected business will not understand that anything at all is happening until some tangible damage has been done. Stuxnet showed the world that a sufficiently skilled and funded attacker could take control of an entire business with only a couple of commands. Given today's corporates' exposure to external networks, Stuxnet certainly points to a deadly prospect.

How To Defend

The best way to protect systems against Stuxnet and other industrial malware is to secure all inbound channels such as removable USB drives and inbound network connections. No USB should be plugged into corporate systems before thorough scanning with updated anti-virus and anti-spyware protection. With the emergence of each threatening zero-day attack, the makers of operating systems produce security patches to secure those vulnerabilities (just as Microsoft came up with patches for all four zero-day vulnerabilities exploited by Stuxnet). All patches for business operating systems should be installed without fail as soon as they become available. The same goes for updates to SCADA systems: It is always wise to install the updates regularly in order to ensure maximum safety.

Once a business system has been infected by industrial malware, it should be disinfected using cleaner software. Quite a few of these programmes became popular for dealing with Stuxnet, but Sysclean from Trend Micro, Stuxnet Rootkit Remover by Greatis Software and Microsoft Security Essentials by Microsoft were the top picks. Any system suspected to be infected by Stuxnet should be scanned, along with any removable drives, with one of these software programmes to remove any infection.

How Attacks Occur:

Procedural Insights

If you are running a business with significant dependence on the computers and external networks, you must already be worried after reading last two chapters! Yes, you got it right! Even your business can be at the receiving end of such mighty blows. But there certainly are ways to make your life less miserable. And as always, charity must begin at home! In order to secure your businesses against cyber attacks, it's important for you to know a few more things about the attacks: how they were carried out, how the worms spread and, most importantly, how you could resist them. Since these worms involve a lot of smart technical innovations, some technical knowledge will be necessary to prevent them. With this particular goal in mind, the information presented here is sufficient to empower a marketer (who, in all probability, doesn't know much about operating systems and computer languages) with some basic technical knowledge so that a business and its computer systems can survive any cyber attack.

Crimeware: Theft of Information and Identity

There was a time when the authors of malicious software (or malware) were interested primarily in notoriety, fame and perhaps anarchy. Unfortunately, those good old days are long gone. The reality on the ground today is completely different. From an early part of the twenty-first century, a notable shift occurred in the cyber-threat landscape. For the first time, hackers and cyber attackers realised that they could potentially reap some serious income from their intrusions. With the number of people conducting online transactions on a steep rise, malicious scripts were no longer just malicious. Now intentions became more criminal than anything else, giving rise to new terminology for a group of malicious software: crimeware. Crimeware is a class of software that executes illegal actions unintended by the user of the software. Often these actions are expected to produce financial benefits for the crimeware's author.

Identity theft is a form of cheating or fraud in which another party assumes someone else's identity without the knowledge or concern of the targeted person. Typically, attackers do this in order to access resources, information or benefits belonging to or authorised only for the original person (e.g., credit card information). A victim (i.e., someone whose identity has been hijacked by the intruder) can suffer a wide array of adverse consequences apart from direct financial or information loss. If the victim is assumed to be accountable for the illegal actions performed by the perpetrator while assuming the victim's identity), then a wide range of adverse consequences may occur. The term *identity theft* was first used back in 1964. Many experts think it is a misnomer, since the crime under consideration is not actually stealing of identity (impossible in a literal sense) but rather identity fraud or illegal impersonation. Even *identity cloning* might be a more appropriate term, but *identity theft* has stuck and is now frequently used by experts and the general public.

Threats from Crimeware: A Business Perspective

In the recent past, a lot of crimeware has been used against corporate rivals, although the majority of cases have been on a small scale. According to a report by United States Department of Homeland Security, the number of keylogger programmes that carries unique signatures is rising almost fourfold per year. The number of sites that actively distribute such crimeware is increasing at an even steeper rate. A huge amount of malware is expected to affect Internet businesses, irrespective of their size. Experts can argue the intentions of crimeware attacks, but from the point of view of business, a cyber-war is definitely on, whether with overly aggressive competitors or with individual hackers looking for personal fortune.

A particular type of crimeware intended to steal classified information from business websites has caused a lot of headaches for the online business community. In severe cases, these data can be used to perpetrate a type of identity fraud commonly called an *identity threat*. Cyber identity theft, in which sensitive data is illicitly obtained from a computer or network and used for commercial profit, is a rapidly growing business itself. Some experts estimate that the direct economic loss due to phishing alone exceeds USD 1 billion each year. But the actual extent of losses is even more severe if account-replacement costs, customer-service expenses and the decreased use of online services owing to public fear about the vulnerability of online financial transactions are all factored in. Crimeware can be utilized to get hold of various kinds of classified information, including passwords and user names, bank account numbers, credit card details, Social Security numbers and personal information (e.g., birth dates, etc.). In addition to misappropriation of customers' online identities, crimeware is also used to execute targeted attacks against corporates such as theft of access to businesses' virtual private networks (VPNs) and theft of business data or intellectual property.

Two different potential uses of stolen identities should worry corporates. First, customers' identities can be faked once some classified information about them is known; for example, an attacker who obtains a customer's bank account number/user name and password can access the customer's account history, opening the door to fraud transactions as well as fraud communications. This can lead to significant business losses. Two of the most publicized and as well as severe payment card breaches in recent times are suspected to have been caused by crimeware. Heartland Payment Systems and RBS Worldpay were the victims of those two attacks. The breach at Heartland remained undetected for no less than six months, compromising more than 100 million cards used for 175,000 merchants. RBS had to acknowledge publicly that the financial data of 1.5 million customers had been lost from its payroll cards business. The stolen card data were in turn used to draw out more than USD 9 million from ATMs across the world. Similar attacks (e.g., the Russian Coreflood Gang attack) also appear to be due to crimeware. Finances are not all that is at stake, however.

The most important loss can be that of reputation. Such breaches are often widely publicized in the media, creating a perception that the transactions involving the company in question lack safety. A lot of customers will stop using the businesses services for fear that the company will not be able to keep their secret information safe.

The other potential application is for an attacker to pretend the identity of the business itself. If some crucial access into the company's internal network can be gained, collecting sensitive information or even crippling operations can be extremely easy. A typical example of this involves theft of passwords and user names for vital systems (e.g., internal mail service, operations control, etc.) of a corporate. A near cousin of this type of attack is phishing, in which an outsider pretends the identity of a service provider and communicates with customers just as the original business does. Fooling customers in this way can be a very easy way to get useful information directly from them.

The scale of the targeted business hardly matters for these attackers. Every prominent business has its fair share of competitors and rivals, however small it may be. Usually, the smaller the scale of a business, the easier an attacker will find breaching their information security. Looking at the track record of identity thieves and the kinds of corporates they have attacked can make anyone with a small Internet business get a shiver down the spine. Moreover, when a large service provider such as a payment gateway is compromised, the breach also affects the thousands of small businesses that use their services. Effectively, every business with some significant operations (e.g., sales, promotion, data maintenance, etc.) is vulnerable to identity theft.

These types of attacks falls into the so-called grey area of the law, as legislation about them are far from well structured. Moreover, tracing back the wrong doer is extremely difficult since they use extremely smart techniques to mask their identities. Once victimized, the legal frontier offers few effective options. When it comes to identity theft, it's best to remember the old saying, "Better safe than sorry."

Types of Attacks and Their Implications for Corporates

Crimeware may come in many different forms. Cyber attackers demonstrate a high degree of technical innovation and reportedly even invest in technology. The most threatening crimeware attacks are always carried out in an organised, near-professional way. As financial institutions and other businesses involving online transactions have increased their online activities, the monetary potential of exploiting account information has hiked many times over. Some attackers such as phishers can afford to invest in regular technology upgrades by virtue of the profits they make from their crimes and illegal actions. Some other hackers may have institutional backing (which funds the launch of attacks on the sponsor's competitors); they too never experience any significant trouble in obtaining technology upgrades. Given the ever-changing spectrum of cybercrime, it's almost impossible to prepare a comprehensive catalogue of prevalent crimeware technologies. Such crimes, instead, must be considered as representative cases. Major types of crimeware that should worry a business with some online presence are:

- Key Loggers and Screen Loggers
  Key loggers are a class of crimeware that gets installed either through a web browser or a device driver. They monitor data inputs by the user and thereafter send the collected data to a phishing server. Key loggers may use various technologies and can be implemented in different ways. A screen logger is a similar programme that tracks both the active portions of the display and the user's inputs to counter security measures involving alternate on-screen input. Key loggers are generally designed to monitor user location and to transmit the information associated with only some specified sites. But the number of such sites may be as large as a few hundred and may include those of payment gateways, banks, information portals, email clients and corporate VPNs (Virtual Private Networks, the connections used for internal communications in different institutions).

  Citing a real world example can be helpful to understanding how such crimeware can affect a corporate. A reputed credit-reporting firm was targeted a few years back via a key logger spread through pornography spam. The spam appeared innocuously in the mail folders of several employees, whose curious clicks enabled the malware to be installed on the company computers. This led to the compromise of more than fifty corporate accounts with access to the firm's internal processes and VPN. These companies in turn were exploited to extract from the agency's internal database no less than 300,000 sets of classified personal information about clients.

Quite evidently, key logger programmes potentially can be used to gain access to the core information and processes of a corporate. They can be used by competitors to extract business secrets, by media houses to find out about dubious practices and by anyone to gain financial benefits by unauthorized transactions.

- Email and Instant Messaging Redirectors

Email redirectors are automated scripts that intercept any email exchange, inbound as well as outbound, and forward a copy to some unintended address, which is accessed by the attacker. Similarly, instant messaging redirectors track chats and instant messages and transmit the transcripts to an outsider.

Instant messaging and email redirectors have been widely used for corporate espionage. What could be a better source of information than a constant feed of all the emails sent by a company's top executives? Competitors can use this type of malware to get access to business secrets, important customer contacts and vital business strategies.

- Session Hijacking

Session hijacking is a class of malware attack in which a remote attacker intrudes and controls a session on a user's computer. In the course of a hijacked session, all user activities are tracked, typically by a malicious component running on the browser. As soon as the user logs into an email account or bank account or initiates an online transaction, this type of malware automatically hijacks the session to secretly execute malicious actions, such as unauthorized transactions, once the user has established identity by providing login and/or verification details. When performed locally by automated software, a hijacked session will look exactly like a legitimate user session that has been initiated from the user's home computer to the targeted site. It can also be used to get hold of information entered on the computer during the session.

Hijacking a session on a competitor's office computers can effectively enable access to the maximum possible amount of information. Hijacking the system of an IT business will reveal all the details of the platforms and techniques it uses and the customers currently served. Hijacking the session of an online merchant will give access to classified information such as supplier contacts, operations details, financial health, etc., and if an attacker is lucky with his timing, he may well skim some direct financial profit by intruding on an online transaction.

- Web Trojans

Web Trojans are controlled by malware that automatically pops up above login screens to collect classified information that proves identity (e.g., user name, passwords, card numbers, date of birth, etc.). A user generally does not recognize that the screen receiving data entries is not as innocuous as it appears to be; what actually happens is that the information is accessed and stored locally and then transferred to the attacker who launched the Trojan.

This is one of the most common types of malware used for identity and/or information theft.

What to Secure: How Is Crimeware Distributed?

It's important to understand how crimeware can infiltrate any network or system. Many people have the misconception that a crimeware infection may happen only by opening an infected file or attachment. But this is just one of the many possible compromise vectors. An infected computer inside a corporate house can spread its infection as an automatically propagating worm, exploiting system vulnerabilities and configurations. A user can become a victim while visiting an apparently trusted website that has put up a compromised or malicious advertisement that works as a crimeware vector. Phishing messages that have external links and shareware that is used for peer-to-peer interaction also can create crimeware infections. Following is a detailed description of the channels usually exploited to distribute crimeware.

- Distribution via Attachments
In this mode of distribution, crimeware is sent as an attachment in emails, instant messaging services or peer-to-peer networks. The most popular practice is to trick a user into opening/downloading the attachment by making it look interesting, by triggering his curiosity (e.g., scandalous video or photos) or practical needs (e.g., a video accelerator codec or a security update). Some attackers prefer to distribute malware by embedding it in a device that is going to be plugged in to the target system (e.g., the smart phone of a corporate executive or an USB flash drive intentionally left near the targeted corporation). Someone who finds such device is very likely to check its ownership by plugging it in to their own computers, which may cause the malware to run automatically.

- Distribution via Piggybacking

Crimeware also may be spread by attaching it with another application that is being intentionally downloaded by a user. Some malicious functionality can be infused in otherwise useful software. Alternatively, malware can be embedded in some software that claims to have useful functionalities or actually has some useful functionality. This is a frequently used mode of propagation for software that causes advertising pop ups (popularly known as adwareand spyware). In a few cases, malicious software also can be installed, with a user's apparent consent, by making him click through lengthy and confusing license agreements that make it incredibly difficult to understand what is being authorised.

- Distribution via Internet Worm

Crimeware can be spread by Internet worms that exploit security vulnerabilities. An infected machine typically will scan to find other vulnerable machines and infect them as well. Worms usually install a backdoor on infected computers, which allows an attacker (either the worm author or an independent or affiliated attacker) to subsequently install crimeware on computers.

- Distribution via Web Browser Vulnerability

Internet browsers are very complex applications and often contain quite a few security holes or vulnerabilities. These vulnerabilities are often exploited to distribute crimeware. When a surfer reaches an infected website, browser vulnerability is exploited by automated scripts on the site. Such security holes may involve processing, parsing, scripting and displaying content, graphics or any other application component that may cause a browser to execute malicious codes. A legitimate site can also spread crimeware payloads via a content-injection attack such as cross-site scripting.

- Distribution via Hacking

Crimeware can also be installed on a target computer by manually exploiting security holes or misconfiguring security features—which is popularly called computer hacking. For obvious reasons, hacking is not a feasible option for massive-scale crimeware attacks, but it can be quite effective when it comes to specific targets, as in case of corporate espionage.
This certainly poses a great risk for businesses, especially bigger ones that have a lot of people using crucial systems. A competitor searching for a way to damage a business website doesn't really need a lot of technical expertise; instead, just managing to get physical access to the company computers, which is not exactly impossible by pulling a string or two with company personnel, will suffice.

When discussing the points of resistance for crimeware attacks, cyber security experts usually talk about infection points (when systems or their security measures are altered) and data-compromise points (when the hacker actually obtains classified information). The following chart is a handy listing of infection points and data-compromise points for the most common crimeware types:

Attack Point	Infection Point	Data-Compromise Point
Key logger/Screen logger	Infection*	Input/Output Device (data entry)***
Session Hijacker	Infection*	Network
Email/IM Redirector	Infection*	Network
Transaction Generator	Infection*	Input/Output Device(data entry)***
Web Trojans	Infection*	External
Hostname Lookup	Execution**	Web Form (data entry)***
Proxy attack	Execution**	Network
Data Theft	Execution**	Storage

* If infection is the infection point, then the computer is compromised as soon as the malware enters the system. Thereafter, it automatically executes all the malicious actions.

** If execution is the infection point, then the computer is not compromised until the application has been started, either by a remote host or by an unsuspecting user.

** * A data entry type of infection point signifies that only the data input by the user is compromised.

To put it precisely, multiple paths into systems and networks must be secured. A business has to ensure the security of the hosting server, all the internal computers and the mail services used by employees as well as the in-house networks. Remember that in this field, best practice is the "defence-in-depth" philosophy: multiple overlapping security measures to avoid severe weaknesses in any one area.

How to Counter Malware: Survival Strategy in Cyberwar

Following are some tried-and-tested measures for curbing identity-theft attacks:

- Anti-viruses
  The first basic step in preventing crimeware is to use a comprehensive, robust, up-to-date anti-virus programme. Installing this anti-virus software on all of a company's enterprise computers is NOT optional. Many antivirus companies provide corporate packages (for different types of businesses), which take care of possible security holes that may lead to corporate espionage attacks. Most cyber experts prefer a complete Internet security package that includes anti-spyware, anti-malware and a robust firewall. For example, Symantec provides two completely different products to provide protection against virus and malware. Similarly, Kaspersky provides both antivirus and total Internet security packages. Installing only the antivirus product will not provide protection against malware and crimeware.

  Nowadays, many companies have done away with client-based virus scanning and only use checks at the email gateways and at the servers. This is a particularly risky practice if you consider the average amount of Internet surfing done from any one enterprise computer. Security packages also should be installed on all other systems that attached to a computer (e.g., mobile phones, PDAs or other gadgets used by employees). Today, various viruses are attacking high-tech gadgets exclusively, and these should not be left unprotected. Regularly updating your security package is also very important. Almost all of them are updated automatically with the automatic update option turned on. But otherwise, make a point of updating manually at least once a day.

- System Patching and Hardening
  Crimeware often spreads like worms once it has found its way into a network. Many types intrude into systems by exploiting configuration weaknesses and common vulnerabilities. For this reason, a business should always ensure the robustness of its computers. It's essential that systems are patched in a regular manner and hardened using a reputed guide such as the one authored by the NSA (National Security Agency) in order to minimize the spread of a crimeware, even if one particular PC gets infected.

A lot of crimeware infections by adware and spyware occur during Internet surfing, All of the major browsers have pop-up blocker and anti-adware features, so it's also important to ensure that the browsers on all enterprise computers are updated as appropriate. Proper care also should be taken to install browser plug-ins. Malicious plug-ins are available in plenty and can result in serious crimeware infections. Some others have security holes that can be easily exploited. Only plug- ins that are absolutely necessary (e.g., AdobeFlash, etc.) should be installed. Peer- to- peer search bars, video-searching toolbars, etc. generally are reported to be more worrying and should be avoided unless necessary.

- Use of Security Plug-ins in the Browser

Some browser plug-ins and add-ons available have basic security features that prevent automatic scripts and adware from infecting computers. Some excellent examples of such add-ons are Flashblock, No Script and Adblock, and there are others. While these are not an essential requirement, they can certainly step up security measures. Before installing such add-ons, however, you should always check their reviews and reputations as malicious add-ons that claim to perform such actions may also exist.

- Data-Leakage Prevention (DLP) Systems

A data leakage prevention system is an enterprise- level security tool that identifies, monitors and protects data at rest (e.g., stored data), in use (e.g., data endpoint actions such as editing or inputting) and in motion (e.g., data transferred through a network or devices). This is achieved by implementing deep and thorough content inspection and contextual security analysis of all the transactions (data object, transfer channel, attributes of originator, destination, timing, etc.). These tools are designed to detect any attempted unauthorised data use and prevent the transmission of confidential information. A DLP continuously monitors network traffic that goes out of a computer, looking for data-transmission or alteration attempts. Although DLP systems are not fool proof, they certainly are a very powerful way to detect and block unauthorized transmission of corporate data for an enterprise that deals with a lot of classified data (e.g., online merchants, transaction gateways and technology-centred services).

- Database and Transport Encryption

Encryption is the cryptographic procedure of transforming raw information (plaintext) using an algorithm (cipher) to make it unreadable to anyone but those who possess special knowledge (the key) about how to decode it. Even if criminals get hold of encrypted data, they cannot make any use of it unless the key is compromised. In the case of data transmission through a network or some device, transport encryption makes it virtually impossible for any outsider to get access. Depending on the scale, nature and use of classified data, a business should consider the option of encrypting database and/or transport channels. Professional service providers offer a wide range of encryption services for businesses. A larger business may want to hire its own specialist for this purpose.

- Increased User Awareness

In many businesses, employees deal directly with data that are classified in the sense that exposure could cause damage to the company. For this reason, it's essential for information-sensitive companies to build awareness among employees on concerns about Internet security. Employees' classes and workshops can be organised to teach safe data-handling practices. Enterprise computer users must understand the sensitivity of the data they are working with and the compliance obligations for handling them. Employees also should be encouraged to take precautions to enforce the organisation's data security.

- Proper Log Monitoring

Continuous and careful log monitoring is fundamental in any satisfactory security programme. Many of the other solutions listed above are merely control mechanisms. If businesses do not keep track of their logs at least once in a day, then crimewares are too difficult to control since a majority can go undetected. Every attack certainly cannot be prevented in this way, but early detection ensures that threats can be taken care of before severe damage occurs. This is especially true in the case of data theft and identity fraud as early detection will deny hackers the time they need to gather information required to build a complex attack.

Basically, to control crimeware in general and identity theft in particular, companies must have a robust, well-secured system in place. At the same time, users' awareness about data security is also very important.

Bot Networks

A botnet is a collection of independent software agents (bots) that can run autonomously and automatically on a remote host computer. Broadly speaking, a bot is an end-user computing machine that uses software that in turn allows it to be controlled by an administrator who is located elsewhere (popularly called a remote administrator) via command and control networks (C&C), frequently from a central server. Practically, the C&C can send all possible instructions to the bot. Commands can be executed without any physical intervention by the human end user on the machine. As a consequence, they can often be executed without the consent or even the knowledge of the end user. The software run by a remote administrator may not necessarily be malicious.

Why to Worry?: A Business Perspective

Initially, most botnets were used for only one purpose: distributed denial-of-service attacks (DDoS, discussed in detail in the next section). Hackers could use them to fight each other for fame and glory in cyberspace. The first well-known use of a DDoS intruder tool was in February of 2000, when a Canadian hacker who nicknamed himself Mafiaboy directed a huge volume of artificially generated traffic to flood many websites. Most of the targets were popular web services such as eBay, CNN.com, Dell computers and Amazon.com. Speaking technically, this was not really a botnet attack, but the practical result was the same. Both online and offline media carried the story, which created panic and gave the hacker even higher status.

Today, the situation is even more severe. Bot networks are often used by determined criminals or corporate rivals. Both use huge bot networks to send phishing mails and spam to innumerable inboxes and to generate click frauds. Click frauds can further be exploited to benefit Internet advertisers or to paralyze rival websites.

Experts say that modern botnets are mostly used to collect classified data for identity fraud, commonly known as identity theft. A modern bot does not just attack other machines; it affects host computers as well. The malware often carries keystroke loggers to extract account numbers, passwords and other secret information. In fact, some smart bots automatically start hunting for financial information, while others have been built solely for the purpose of gathering PayPal accounts, online banking passwords, credit card numbers and all kinds of personal information from compromised hosts. Professional hackers also use botnets to run click frauds. Google's anti-fraud system is robust enough to detect and terminate thousands of clicks emanating from just one computer, but it's much harder to know whether a single click by thousands of computers is fraud or just sheer popularity. This dilemma poses severe concerns for all online ad providers or for anyone related to online ad businesses.

Alarmingly, bots do not only compromise the actions of the computer they have broken into; at the same time, they constantly search for other machines that can be infected and added to the bot network. In 2011, *Dutch Daily News* reported (quoting research by T. U. Delft) that no less than 10 percent of all the computers in the country were part of botnets. In 2005, Dutch police discovered and terminated a 1.5-million-node bot network. The case of a number of other countries, especially the developing ones, may be similar when it comes to botnets. Botnets pose an immense threat to all businesses in general, and to data-driven ones (e.g., banking services, e-businesses, etc.) in particular, as there is huge risk of compromising classified information in bulk.

What makes these botnets especially threatening is the fact that modern bot networks can be upgraded, even by remote administrators. Operators can add new functionalities to their bots as they wish and can even switch from one bot to another. It has been generally observed that bot authors regularly upgrade their codes, even after release, in order to evade detection by malware cleanup tools or anti-virus programmes.

With the ever-evolving botnet attacks, anti-virus vendors are hard-pressed to stay ahead in the fight against botnet infections. Recent botnets have also shown an inclination for staged operation. For example, a computer may first be infected by malware. By the time an antivirus programme finds and neutralizes the malware, it already will have downloaded the next phases of the infection. Finally, the botnet will delete even the original infected file, making it hard for anti-virus programmes to find them. Another botnet defence is to disable antivirus engines in order to remain undetectable.

How To Play Safer

Experts think that large businesses and Internet Service Providers (ISPs) still have a lot to catch up on when it comes to internal botnet infections. The number of measures (such as DNS blacklists) tracking botnets is severely insufficient, and this certainly is not the greatest news for victims' businesses. Detecting bots in-house definitely takes a lot of expertise and vigilance and entails recognizing the patterns present in a large number of emails and recognizing harmful bots in incoming items. Office mail servers should be configured to detect the details required to single out messages that originate with bots.

To detect bots, start with blocking incoming as well as outgoing traffic (especially those via e.g. port 25), although corporates also must ensure that they don't end up blocking their internal mail servers). Using a good firewall, preferably from a vendor who specializes in corporate security, is also mandatory. Firewall logs should be checked from time to time to see if any intruder system is trying to spam from some other network. You should also be alarmed if the number of DNS (Domain Name System) queries (a hierarchical list of hostnames and IP addresses accessed) is on the higher side, as bots usually result in many more DNS enquiries than usual. Keeping an eye on the .ru, .info, .cn and MX lookups is also a good idea. These lookups usually signify attempted communication between bots and a command-and-control server.

TCP (Transmission Control Protocol) fingerprinting is another technique to keep tabs on potential bot attacks. TCP is the core protocol of the Internet protocol suite, used by practically all computers to connect to Internet networks. TCP provides for ordered delivery of byte streams carrying encoded information from one computer to another. By fingerprinting (i.e., tracking) the TCP, it is possible to search for already known botnets (e.g., Srizbi). TCP fingerprinting can also provide some useful information about the remote device.

Large organisations tend to assume that anti-virus engines will catch botnet infestations, but most of the time they don't. Some botnets are so good at hiding that running an anti-virus scan frequently will gives a PC a clean bill of health, while behind the scenes the botnet is still operating smoothly.

Several cyber-security firms such as Symantec, Afferent Security Labs, FireEye, Trend Micro, Damballa and Umbra Data have announced security packages to stop botnets. Most of these services are targeted to protect enterprises and/or Internet Service Providers (ISPs). These services incorporate either a host-based or a network-based approach. Host-based techniques use heuristics (an experience-based approach) to identify bot behaviors that could have bypassed a conventional anti-virus scan. A network-based approach tries to curb botnet activities by shutting down C&C servers/IRC servers, null routing DNS entries, etc.

DDoS (Distributed Denial of Service)

Who has never experienced a busy telephone line while trying to make an urgent call? This may happen on a major holiday or on a day such as Mother's Day or Valentine's Day, when a lot of people try to make phone calls. In fact, in the early days of telecommunications, telephone companies in the United States used to advertise urging customers to avoid the peak hours by calling early or late in the day. These blockages happen because the telephone system is capable of handling only a certain call volume at any given time. Computer systems also experience a similar problem. Network computers are designed to handle a certain volume of users at a time. If an exceptionally large number of users surf a website at the same time, the website server may well go down. This experience is not uncommon. Very recently, www.kyazoonga.com (an online merchant dealing with tickets and passes) went down soon after the sale of World Cup Cricket tickets started, as millions of fans tried to book their tickets as soon as possible.

Websites in this state are particularly vulnerable. If an attacker can overload a website by artificially boosting the number of visitors, even for a very short time, the website will effectively crumble. This type of attack is called a denial-of-service (DoS) attack. As the intruder will be required to pump up the number of visitors as high as possible, it also may be called a distributed denial-of-service (DDoS) attack.

Types of DDoSs: How Do Attacks Occur?

DDoS attacks can first be classified on the basis of the intruder's intention. The following classes of attacks are possible:

- Intrusion
  Intrusion, the most innocuous of a computer hacker's possible intentions, refers to old-school attacks done more to prove the hacker's prowess than with the intention of doing any major harm. The hacker may take personal satisfaction in bypassing the security measures of a site, thereby also earning prestige within the hacking community. This type of attack may well come with a notice declaring that the site has been hacked. At times, such hackers even leave details of bugs in the system that allowed entry and how to counter them. While intrusion may not cause any severe damage to the system, it can hinder a website's service and thus its overall reputation among customers.
- Disruption
  An attacker's major aim may be to disrupt the service rendered by a website, possibly as a tactic to disrupt a competitor's business. For instance, pulling down the website of a competitor when a special offer or new promotional drive is on can do a lot of harm. If a website's server is hung down with an overload of surfers, restoring normal service might take quite some time, which is even more threatening to business. Effectively, a hacker's misdeed sustained for only a short time can result in a crippling effect that lingers for much longer.
- Information Threat
  Some attacks are for the purpose of gaining access to information that is otherwise restricted. The targeted information is often sensitive and regarded as a business secret (e.g., customer contacts, transaction histories, card numbers and even passwords). This type of attack is particularly threatening for any business that provides a platform for online transactions. If the information such as card numbers and passwords are ever compromised, a great deal of damage can be done to customers, and this in turn can completely destroy the reputation of a company. A malintentioned competitor can use even relatively less-classified information such as customer contacts to lure the customers away through target-marketing campaigns.
- Modification

In some instances, attackers have actively altered the information on websites or their underlying processes. An altered website can damage a reputation like nothing else. What could be worse than a website that acquires links to a page that describes how bad a company's products are? More dangerously, if critical processes such as payment making and ordering can be altered, then the whole operation of a website may be forced into a virtual dead end. Another particularly annoying aspect of these kinds of attacks is their concealment, which makes it very difficult to spot and correct the misdeed. Any online sales or promotion website should be particularly cautious about such attacks.

A number of vulnerable attack points, if utilized, could crumble a web server, making it inaccessible to normal clients. DDoS attacks may fall into this classification, depending upon the part of a computer system that they target. A DDoS can attack any one of the following:

- <u>Client Websites</u>: Attacking a client site directly is possibly the oldest form of DDoS attack. As with other cyber crimes, procedures have now progressed much further. For the moment, direct client attacks are infrequent, mainly because major business websites have already taken enough precautions. Instead, the routers that connect host webservers to the Internet Service Providers (ISPs) now present a reasonable starting attack point. An attack of this kind effectively cuts down Internet access to servers, making them inaccessible.
- <u>Firewall Systems</u>: Another common target of DDoS attacks are firewall systems. Although firewalls generally are quite immune to direct attack (or should be), they remain a popular target because of the resultant impact. A firewall functions something like a bottleneck through which all outbound and inbound traffic must pass. As a result, any increase in traffic experienced by a firewall will have at least a twofold impact: An attack that effectively involves increasing traffic to a very high volume may stop a firewall from working properly; the firewall will then block most in- and outbound traffic, thus limiting the site's accessibility
- <u>Load Balancers</u>: A load balancer is an arrangement designed to save networks from DDoS attacks. To put it simply, a load balancer distributes a network's workload between different servers at different physical locations. Load balancers have been attacked in the recent past with the intention of crippling a server's security measures and then hanging it up. Experts predict that load balancers will be major future targets of attacks as more and more sites incorporate them.
- <u>Individual Web Servers</u>: Individual web servers also can be targets, but attacks on them are expected to be less severe, since most major sites are hosted from multiple servers. Some advanced attacks may try to overload all of them all at the same time, and in such a case, impacts will be much higher than with a single-server attack. Web servers are particularly vulnerable because they chiefly use commercially available (off-the-shelf) hardware and software whose details and flaws attackers can very easily access.

Implication for Businesses

As mentioned earlier, DDoS attacks are probably the worst possible threat for a business. Using DDoS to cripple the website of an online vendor is the cyber equivalent of breaking into a store or a mall and destroying its goods. Annoyingly, aggressive competitors can use DDoS as a measure to ensure a competitor's website is down when a special sale is going on or during peak sales seasons. Even for businesses other than online merchants, DDoS is a major worry. If a buyer tries to visit your website but can not load, the resulting impression is bad and may prompt a visit to another website offering similar information or service. A hacker also can alter some crucial Internet content and cause major embarrassment for a business, if not even more serious complications.

Interrupted service is not the only possible result of a DDoS attack that should worry businesses. An attacker can also steal sensitive business information (e.g., customer contacts or even more dangerously, passwords and credit card data). This can be of particular concern for online-transaction platforms as compromised data can cause a lot of worry and complications for customers and destroy a business's reputation. Businesses have abundant reasons to be on high alert when it comes to DDoS attacks.

How Does DDoS work?

A DDoS attacker generally starts by building a network of computers that can be utilized to generate the large volume of traffic required to deny services to real users. This network of computers is commonly called an attack network. For this purpose, intruders generally look for poorly secured computers: the ones that are not properly patched or that lack up- to-date security systems (anti-viruses, anti-spyware, etc.). When the attacker identifies such computers, the next step is to install on them software and scripts that will facilitate remote control of the selected computers to carry out attacks. Nowadays the process of selecting attack computers has also been automated and is typically carried out by self-propagating programmes that automatically search for vulnerable machines, intrude on them and install the required software. Thereafter, these compromised computers start looking for new computers with vulnerable security systems. Once a DDoS programme is installed on a computer, it identifies all other computers with the same programme as members of its network. This self-propagating feature of DDoS programmes results in a large network build in a short amount of time. Before too long, all of these compromised computers can be used to generate a huge volume of traffic to a targeted website. Many computer security experts believe that a huge number of such attack networks currently exist. Many are believed to be dormant, i.e., passively waiting for instructions to launch DDoS attacks against targets. Opinion is divided, however; other experts think that most attacks are launched soon after a network has been built and a victim site has been identified.

To do away with any chance of discovering their identities, attackers typically distribute their traffic volume across various system administrators, time zones and legal jurisdictions (i.e., different countries and states). Expert attackers also make the high-volume website traffic their networks create appear to be from computers other than the ones that actually generate it. This technique, known as IP spoofing, has been widely used in the recent past to disguise the true generators of virtual traffic. Without any knowledge about the source of an attack, curbing it becomes difficult, giving the attackers a high likelihood of successful intrusion while remaining anonymous.

In the recent past, a wide variety of attack techniques have caught major business websites on the wrong foot. A classic example of such an attack is the MyDoom worm. MyDoom (or W32.MyDoom@mm) emerged in the early part of 2004 and affected Microsoft Windows. This worm provides an example of how DDoS attacks are actually executed. MyDoom's attack network was built by exploiting operational vulnerabilities instead of common technological deficiencies. Computer users were cajoled into running malware propagated as email attachments or as files downloadable via a point-to-point network connection. This malware was DDoS software that ultimately enrolled compromised computer systems into the attack network. In the case of MyDoom, however, these systems were not remotely controlled through the newly installed malware. Instead, the malware programme was designed to automatically generate large amounts of traffic to various websites, first to www.sco.com (1 February 1 2004) and then to www.microsoft.com (3 February 3 2004).

Countering DDoS: Prevention Is Better than Cure

No effective, proven short-term solution can completely do away with DDoS attacks. Experts all around the world agree that best practice is to make computers and networks more resilient against such attacks. When it comes to facing DDoS attacks, survivability should be the major point of focus. All hosting systems have their upper limits of traffic handling. The simplest way of making a system more robust is to better these limits. The more resources used to back up the hosting server, the better the chance that the system will not fail, even amidst overloading traffic volume. Just like telephone companies, who add more circuits and towers to increase their call-handling capacities, a webmaster should increase the number of network connections that a website can accept. This can be done in various ways; one would be by adding more web servers. This allows any increased traffic to be dealt with through a number of computers, thus ensuring that none of the servers gets pushed above its limit. The higher the combined capacity of all the host servers, the better is the odds that a DDoS-targeted website will survive a severe attack.

Another effective way to counter DDoS attacks is to implement some failover techniques. Failover is the ability to switch automatically to a standby server, computer system or network once the previously active application or system fails or terminates abnormally. Generally, human intervention is not required in the process of failover. Instead, it automatically happens as soon as a failure occurs, just like switchover in electrical systems. In the case of major websites, webmasters should incorporate failover capability in servers to create a high degree of reliability in case of attack. In the case of servers, an automated failover process is implemented using a "heartbeat" cable to connect two or more servers. As long as the normal pulse or heartbeat between the active and backup servers is maintained, the backup servers remain in a dormant or passive state. The backups will immediately take over, however, as soon as they stop receiving pulses from the active server for a sustained period of time. For websites handling exceptionally large traffic, a set of "spare parts" servers may also be installed to run extra components for "hot" switching (i.e., very quick switchover) to prevent long down time. Virtualization software has been used to make the failover process less dependent on hardware.

A few specialized techniques have also been proposed to deal with DDoS attacks including the center track approach, the controller agent technique, graphic turing tests, etc. The effectiveness of such approaches is yet to be tested beyond doubt, and they are too complex to be implemented by anyone but an expert.

Implementing DDoS protection may turn out to be extremely costly if a business buys the necessary equipment itself, particularly for small e-commerce projects. For this reason, shared DDoS services have proved attractive in the recent past. A number of providers buy protective equipment and use it to provide safe hosting for a number of small websites as a shared service. Shared DDoS protection service has also got some bad press lately. Many experts feel that this was mainly due to ignorance and the spread of false information, for instance, the belief that if any site on the shared server gets attacked, then it will affect all of the other sites hosted on the same server. This need not be true, however, if service providers keep each part of each web account, from the IP (on the network level) to the CPU and Ram (on the server level), isolated from each other. With this precaution, if one website account exceeds its resource allocation (protection limit), that website will be isolated and null routed by the protection service. With this isolation technique, overloading of a particular website will not affect other sites hosted on the server. Another serious allegation against shared-service providers is that they may fatten up traffic data to skim extra charges from their customers. Needless to say, running a thorough check and reviewing conditions before opting for any such service is strongly advisable.

In short, the only way to curb DDoS attacks on a business website is to make the host system more robust by growing its capacity to handle increased traffic volume. Hosting the site from more than one server or opting for a reputable shared DDoS-protection service may significantly help in this cause.

How To Win a Cyberwar

In the last chapter we have discussed some of the specific measures that should be taken for businesses to guard against different types of attacks. But those certainly are not the end of the road in cyber defence. Some generic safe-cyber practices and security techniques can help businesses emerge unaffected from the threatening scenario of corporate cyberwar. The absolute basics shared here are musts for all businesses, and the wise ones will ensure that they stick to them without fail. In addition, some businesses may need specific security guidelines, such as those discussed in the previous chapter, for particular types of attacks.

Deter, Detect, Defend

The Federal Trade Commission, a U.S. agency that works for consumer protection, has advised a three-stage process to ensure security against identification thefts and frauds. This process is called the Deter, Detect and Defend methodology. While there may be no foolproof method to completely stop identity fraud, specific steps can and should be taken to minimize risk and damage if a theft should occur. The primary intention of the DDD methodology is to make it tougher for thieves to steal identities, and the FTC's guidelines are expected to be useful for both individuals and corporates, especially smaller businesses that cannot afford to employ a full-fledged cyber-security team.

The first step in this defence methodology is to deter identity and information thieves by securing all sensitive information. Many data such as documents kept on a hard disc, business email exchanges, and passwords, PINs and credit card numbers entered on web forms can be accessed by hackers. All of these must be safeguarded if the goal is to put them out of the reach of cyber attackers. Some suggestions to follow are:

- Make a point of not giving out personal information over the Internet (e.g., through an e-mail) unless the real identity and trustworthiness of the receiver is absolutely certain. Banks and credit card companies will never ask for personal information via emails. Any links that invite visitors to enter classified information should start with "https," which signifies an HTTP secure protocol. While using a public wireless connection in a coffee shop or airport, try not to use or disclose sensitive personal (especially financial) information.
- Do not click on any link sent in an unsolicited email; this can lead to a number of troubles including automated crimeware installations, infection through cookies that can lead to compromise of sensitive information entered in a browser window, and so on. Even if the link looks like a website that you trust, type the link in the address bar before completing the requested action. Unsolicited links may lead to a false website and compromise of identity.
- Use anti-virus programmes, anti-spyware and firewalls to protect office and home or personal computers. Set browser settings to always ask before allowing a download. Updating protection programmes regularly is also strongly advisable. If using peer-to-peer networks to share files, check to ensure that no sensitive documents or files are shared.
- For systems, secured files, emails and accounts, never use obvious passwords such as digits from a phone number/social security number, date of birth, mother's maiden name, etc. In addition, use numbers, symbols and letters in both upper and lower case in passwords. Using a variety of characters helps increase password strength, making it more difficult to crack.
- Be aware that manual misappropriation of data also occurs. Only a limited number of trusted employees should be allowed to access a company's sensitive information, with special attention to who should be allowed access to databases through networks.

- For extremely sensitive information such as vital financial details or core business strategies, proper encryption might be wise if such information is kept on company computers. Even if attackers get hold of some encrypted data, they won't be able to read it.

The second to-do level of protection involves detecting any suspicious activity early enough to stop significant information theft. For this, it's essential to monitor all company networks, documents, systems and financial accounts regularly. As soon as something alarming appears, take immediate action to restrict further damage. Some suggestions to abide by include:

- Keep regular track of all system network logs. Watch out for any unauthorised data in movement, or any unauthorized or unplanned connection. This will ensure that no bot is transmitting secret information over unauthorized networks. Regular log checks can block a large number of attacks as most will leave a mark on the network log when transmitting information to a remote attacker.
- Also watch out for any unexpected change in credit card or account statements. Be careful if any passwords suddenly appear to have changed and can no longer be used to log in to an account with an old password any more.
- Also keep an eye on the integrity of files and the kernel. Many attacks alter the normal functioning of a system's kernel. A files and kernel integrity-management system can certainly help in this regard.
- For all accounts (e.g., emails, financial services, etc.), enable the option to receive text messages when passwords or any other major details have changed. This will help you to track any unauthorized changes to login details

The next step is to defend against any identification/ information theft as soon as it is identified. The aim is to minimize damage if it has already started or, if has yet to start, stop it altogether. Remember:

- Any network connection on a system that is believed to be unauthorized could be responsible for data hijacking and should be turned off immediately.
- Any account suspected to be compromised should be reported immediately to the service provider and the login details changed.
- Compromised accounts may need to be closed down, especially financial accounts such as credit cards.
- If the fraud is a major concern, report it to the police or appropriate governing body (e.g., the Federal Trade Commission in the United States).

If some data theft has already occurred, not much can be done to prevent attackers from using it, so it's extremely important to prepare security strategies well and detect any attempted theft before real damage can be done.

How To Get Rid of Phishing and Other Email Worries

E-mail is certainly the preferred communication method of this century. But the convenience of email's instant reach, permanent storage and minimal cost can cause a few worries. Spam and phishing are major email problems. Spam does not pose a big threat for most businesses. Spam can flood inboxes and annoy staff, but it's probably not going to cause a business disaster. With insufficient caution, however, phishing emails can be a real threat. Phishing usually carry details that look like some websites that employees recognize and trust—a credit card company, a bank or a trusted partner's website, for instance—but will lead to compromise of information upon entry. These scams often reach their greatest heights after national disasters, such as the major earthquake in Japan in 2011. Other email threats include messages that contain attachments or links that will install malware automatically on systems. As for possible protections, quite a few steps may be taken to sidestep the deceits propagated by phishing emails.

<u>Open Emails Wisely</u>

All emails that have been reported as malicious have a few common features. Knowing these features and identifying all emails that look suspicious will make it possible to avoid most of the trouble they hold in store.

- Most malicious emails are sent to a lot of people at the same time. A long list of email IDs in the Sent field should be a red-flag reminder not to point to or click on any link or download any attachment. Even if the email is from someone known, there is always a possibility that the ID was hacked before the mail was sent.
- A lot of suspicious emails have very catchy subjects or texts: something scandalous or erotic, a free update or software, etc. The receipt of such unexpected "gifts" should raise the alarm and give cause for thorough checking. Dubious keywords (such as Viagra, naked, mortgage, pharmacy, etc.) may also be added to the keyword filter, so that all the mails containing these words will automatically be sent to a spam folder. Spammers will also try to make their way into inboxes by changing keywords a little (e.g., Vi@gr@ for Viagra). By looking out for these patterns, more words can be selected for keyword filtering. Unfortunately, some spam will always get through, and in the same way, some non-spam mails will be marked as spam. Spam mails should always be sent to a spam folder instead of automatically deleted. Missing something important from a trusted broker just because he used the word *mortgage* is not the result most business people are after!
- Embedded links are the most dangerous weapon of any phisher. An email scam leading to identity thefts will hardly work without them. Here's why: There are two aspects of a link embedded in some text or email: the real URL (the intended website address) and what the embedded link reads. You must have seen a clickable link that reads something else (e.g., a link on a mail that read, "Click here for a huge discount!". In the same way, anyone with devious intentions can easily change a normal link's appearance to something catchy and attractive. And, of course, it's possible to mask the real URL with something more trustworthy. For example, a link to a malicious phishing website can be masked as "www.paypal.com". Now, Paypal is something many of us do trust, but clicking on this particular unsolicited link will only lead to exposure to information theft. This is the reason why computer users should employ Tooltip, a GUI (graphical user interface) that works along with a mouse pointer. With Tooltip, a view of the actual link will appear as soon as the mouse cursor hovers over the link before it is clicked, a valuable piece of information for avoiding links in disguise.
- It's advisable to type all website addresses on the address bar, especially those involving classified information, rather than relying on clicks. Before entering any financial or other sensitive details, make sure that the URL starts with *https* instead of only *http*. Never enter

any classified information when using an unsecured public network (such as in a coffee shop).

When it comes to email threats, the moral of the story remains simple: Do not click anything that looks dubious or even unexpectedly lucrative. Until a malicious download option or a link is clicked, information and identity remains safe.

Encryption To Stop Hacking

Put simply, encryption is the procedure of encoding classified information in such a way that only the person (or system) that knows the "key" can decode and read it. Transport Layer Security (TLS) and Secure Sockets Layer (SSL) are the two most frequently used cryptographic protocols used to ensure security of communications over the Internet. SSL and TLS encrypt various segments of network connections using symmetric cryptography.

A computer needs a structured algorithm to encrypt and decipher information. An encryption algorithm provides the methodology for transforming plaintext (i.e., raw data) into so-called ciphertext (i.e., encrypted data). An encrypted piece of information is unintelligible to anyone who is unaware of the secret key required to decipher it. The process of data encryption has its origin in Greek history (sometime around 500 B.C.), when kings and generals used to send messages to colleagues and allies through secret codes. Until the advent of modern computing, data encryption was the exclusive territory of armies and academics. Nowadays, encryption methods are routinely used to secure classified databases, online banking and credit card services, customer information, digital rights management and even sensitive email exchanges.

Methods of Encryption

Encryption algorithms can be broadly classified in two groups, symmetric and asymmetric. An Encryption algorithm is referred to as symmetric when it uses the same key (or password) for both encryption and decryption. An asymmetric encryption algorithm uses different keys for encryption and decryption.

Symmetric encryption is the oldest and most popular technique. A secret key (which can be something as simple as a word), a string of random letters or a number is used to change a text, message or data in a particular pre-specified way. A very simple example of this is a text message that has been encrypted by shifting each and every letter by a certain number of places in the alphabet. In this case, the key is simply the number of places used for the shift. For this procedure to work, both the sender and receiver have to know the key so that they can encrypt and decrypt messages by using it. The problem with symmetric encryption lies in its vulnerability. Preventing the secret keys from falling into the wrong hands if they are exchanged over a large network (e.g., the Internet) is almost impossible. Anyone can get hold of the key by breaking into the network or by stealing it from one of the systems involved. Once someone has both the key and the message, it is not possible to prevent the message from being read.

This problem inspired cryptographers to invent the asymmetric encryption technique. This method generates a pair of related keys. One is a "public key," which is freely available to anyone who may want to send a classified message. The other "private key" is a secret that only the recipient of the message will know. Any file (a message/binary file/text/document/data, etc.) can be encrypted by applying the public key. Decryption, however, requires the matching private key. Asymmetric decryption removes the worry about keys leaking to unwanted people. Public keys can be passed to anyone, as they are meant to be public. The private key, of course, must be kept in a safe place. The flipside of the asymmetric encryption technique is its relatively slower speed and greater need for processing power.

To use an asymmetric encryption algorithm, there has to be a way to allow people to discover others' public keys. Generally, digital certificates (also just called certificates) are used for this purpose. A certificate is a specified pack of information that helps identify a server or user. Typically, a digital certificate contains vital information such as the name of the organisation to which it belongs, the name of the certificate-issuing organisation, the location and email address of the user, and, of course, the public key of the user. When server and client require secure encrypted communication, they send a query over the network to the other party, which sends back a copy of the certificate. The other party's public key can be extracted from the certificate. A certificate can also be used to uniquely identify the holder.

How Is Encryption Used?

For most business owners, data encryption is too complex to execute without help. For those who are worried about their classified information and/or emails, the options are to build a team of in-house professionals or to hire an encryption service provider. Developing a dedicated team is resource and time intensive and not feasible for most small businesses. The best bet is to look for a suitable provider. A lot of firms provide encryption services for data and email, some of the most famous being LANSA Codestart, CRYPO, zixCorp and Microsoft Exchange Hosted Encryption.

Businesses using online payment gateways should make sure to use https links instead of simple http links. The idea behind HTTPS is to create a secure data-transmission channel over an insecure network. This results in satisfactory protection from man-in-the-middle attacks and eavesdroppers, provided that the required cipher suites are implemented and that server certificates from trusted issuers are also verified. Paying attention to browser warnings about outdated/untrusted security certificate for websites is a must.

Security against Website Hacking

Many webmasters don't even realise that their websites have been hacked. Here is a handy checklist of symptoms:

- If the results pages of any search engine, especially Google or Yahoo, show warnings about the company website (e.g., "This site may harm your computer"), then there is a good chance that the website has been hacked.
- If the company web pages suddenly come up with texts, links or any other objects that the company didn't put there, this is an indication that the site has been hacked. The source codes of web pages (e.g., the text in your .php, .html or .htm file) should always stay as it was when it was created. If it changes, this is a red alert that someone has figured out how to break into your site.

- If visitors to the website automatically get taken to another website instead, this too is a symptom of being hacked. Eventually, these redirections will earn your site a "badware flag" from Yahoo or Google.
- A lot of services are available to check whether websites are hack free. These include Norton Safe Web, StopBadware.org clearinghouse database (which will even provide a short summary of any malware found in checking a website) and McAfee SiteAdvisor software. Make a point of checking the company website's status regularly using these tools.

Most websites, fortunately, do not get hacked. When it does happen, usually something is wrong with the webhost, the server, the site itself or a computer's security. When hacking does occur, the damaged files must not only be cleaned and repaired but the cause of the breach must be determined. Only then will the company site be safe from a repeat hacking incident.

If the company website definitely has been hacked, follow this basic task list:

- As a first step, log into the website control panel (e.g., cPanel or Plesk) and check for any unauthorized logins. Also check the HTTP and FTP logs to find out the IPs responsible for the attacks. Probably this won't reveal anything about the identity of the attackers, most of whom are automated robots, but it may yield useful information about how the attack was carried out.
- Report the hacking incident to the site's webhosting company and include information about the intruder IPs. Many webhosts will help investigate hacking incidents and even clean up hacked sites. Even if the hosting company does not offer such services, its advice will always be helpful.
- In 2009, experts say, hackers most often gained access to websites via the webmaster's personal computer. Using malware, attackers stole FTP login information from the webmasters and sent it off to remote computers, from where victims' website pages could be loaded up with JavaScript or hidden iframes. This modus operandi points to malicious websites such as gumblar.cn, martuz.cn and many others on an ever-expanding list. The lesson is that webmasters, especially, must be diligent about checking their own computers with anti-virus and anti-spyware software.
- Once the administrator systems have been cleaned of malware and viruses, all of the website passwords used for all components related to webhosting—including FTP, control panel, email and database connections—must be changed. Choose strong passwords, and ensure that passwords that may have been used for more than one purpose are also replaced.
- The next task is to make a list of all third-party scripts that have been used on the hacked website and upgrade each one to its latest version.
- Finally, examine PHP or ASP.NET codes for security holes. Then, find and repair all the malicious changes that were made during the hack.

Whether a website has been hacked or not, here are a few steps to take in order to ensure its future security:

- Maintain robust security on each of the PCs that are used to manage a website. Install up-to-date anti-virus software and patch the operating system regularly.
- Follow the accepted best website practices. Chief among these: Use passwords of sufficient strength, i.e., with eight to twenty upper case/lower case/numeric/punctuation characters in a random combination.

- Avoid the temptingly cool scripts, gadgets, features, functions, and code snippets so freely available on the web. For a secure website, use only carefully chosen third-party scripts, and only after reading and understanding their vulnerability reports (available at Secunia.com).
- Keep all third-party scripts up to date.
- Don't weaken the server's file and folder permissions.
- Always keep a backup copy of the company's entire website and its databases. This will make further diagnosis, cleanup and repairs much easier if they are ever needed.
- A site's raw HTTP and FTP logs are an important source of information after an attack. Normally, these are deleted at regular intervals, usually once a day. Enable archiving (by turning on "log archiving" in the cPanel), allowing them to accumulate and preserve the evidence after an attack. Periodically download and review these logs to see what kinds of attacks are being launched against the website. If the logs are taking up a lot of disc space, delete the oldest ones periodically.
- Use good database connection practices in the scripts used. And don't forget to put the MySQL connection data in a well-secured file.
- To add extra layers of security, consider blocking suspicious activities (e.g., bad robots, suspicious URL query strings, etc.) with .htaccess

Password-Related Issues

Good Password Selection

Passwords may seem very basic, but choosing easily guessable passwords or using the same passwords for many accounts are common mistakes that many people make. Selecting the same user names and passwords for each and every account *does* make them easier to remember—but that's the only advantage of this practice. The risks, on the other hand, are very grave; using the same password for all accounts can potentially open up all of an individual or company's cyber secrets in a single blow. Try to vary at least a few characters in passwords used for the important accounts (e.g., primary email account, bank account, corporate VPN account, etc.). Using easy-to-guess passwords (such as dates of birth, phone numbers, Social Security numbers, wife's/mother's name, etc.) is a strict no-no. To make passwords more robust, introduce complexity by adding alpha-numeric characters, capital and small letters, etc. Not only accounts, but also corporate as well as personal computers, PDAs and smartphones, should be password protected. Passwords also can be used to protect classified data and documents. (Even very popular software such as Adobe Professional enables this.) Many companies today also rotate passwords. This would be advisable, as the frequent change limits damage if one is compromised.

Password Recovery

Set your password recovery parameters wisely. All major email service providers, online financial services and shopping websites have their own standard procedures for password recovery. Some allow changes to passwords via mail sent to an alternative email address or a text message sent to the account holder's phone. Others may require contacting their customer support department with proof of identity. Be sure to know these procedures and set the alternative email accounts/phone numbers correctly. This will enable recovery of forgotten passwords without delay. If forgotten passwords are a frequent problem in the workplace, reputable password recovery software is commercially available. Always remember that saving passwords in any readable format is always a no-go, whatever the circumstances.

Epilogue

No business can have prior knowledge of every move its rivals make. Similarly, it is impossible to know whether anyone is planning a cyber assault on a company until an attack actually has been unleashed. The wisest policy is to always adhere to the safe cyber practices discussed at length in the previous chapters. Still, it's always good to have a quick guide as a reminder. So, in the spirit of good defence against cyber threats, here is a list of ten absolutely basic security measures that should always be followed:

1. Don't take anti-virus protection lightly. Anti-virus software is the single most important security tool at your disposal. Use a trusted anti-virus programme, and always keep it updated
2. Don't forget to patch systems with all of the latest releases from software vendors, especially the makers of computer operating systems.
3. Carefully monitor logs from time to time. These will reveal whether unauthorized connections are active from the system.
4. Every time a web form requests sensitive information such as passwords or credit card numbers, look at the URL in the browser's address bar. Make sure that it's the site you trust and not a phishing link.
5. Don't download attachments or click on the links in an email from an unknown source. These attachments may contain malware or links that can prompt automatic download of malware.
6. Keep passwords long and difficult to guess. Mix alphanumeric characters, capital and small cases, symbols and numbers. Don't use the same password everywhere.
7. Regularly check websites for infection by worms or hacking. If anything has gone wrong, check the web administrator's cPanel, inform the hosting service provider, scan the administrator systems, update all the third-party scripts, remove scripts that are non-essential and, of course, clean up infections.
8. Maintain websites at a satisfactorily large traffic-handling capacity. If average traffic volume is on the higher side, maintain two or more servers with failover mechanisms implemented between them.
9. Consider encrypting the most classified data. Strictly use https links to carry out Internet transactions.
10. Keep all employees well informed about safe practices. The more classified information is, the fewer people should have access to it. Keep an eye on all corporate computers.

In addition to these basic measures, you may need additional layers of security to prevent specific attack techniques, as discussed in the previous two chapters. Consider the above as the Ten Commandments of Cyber Security. Ignore them at your own risk!

Most businesses of today will be more than happy to simply secure their infrastructure against the potential cyber attacks of tomorrow. Only a very few big corporations can dare to think of cyber espionage involving teams of dedicated hackers trying to get into the websites and computers of rival businesses—and then come the legal and moral complexities of being involved in such activities. For most businesses when it comes to cyberwar, winning is synonymous with surviving. For those who are knowledgeable and prepared, surviving is not such a steep task. Defending proactively—that is, taking the measures needed to secure cyber assets, instead of waiting to clean up the mess after an attack—is always advisable. With the cyber-threat scenario changing continuously and new threats evolving over time, it's important to remember that cyber systems can never be 100-percent fool-proof. Defences can be strengthened, but they will not necessarily be impermeable.

The Greek war schools were pioneers in analyzing war strategy. At a time when trade routes were defined by muscle power, the Greeks started making note of their opponents' strengths and weaknesses, specialties and peculiarities. Greek generals learned their lessons from these analyses and went back to the field of war knowing that they would not be repeating their previous mistakes. As a result, the Greeks not only built an empire across the continents, but also prospered in trade and business. In today's world of cyber insecurities, businesses need to follow the same strategy as the Greek generals, trying their best to be proactive and building forts before the next assaults come. Unfortunately, no one call tell with certainty what the next attack will look like. Business leaders must also learn from each new attack and prepare accordingly. Most importantly, businesses must always stay on their toes in order to recover quickly after confronting the unknown.

The wisest businesses are always prepared before the storm arrives. By starting preparations right now, securing systems in all possible ways, your business can emerge a winner in the next corporate cyberwar!